Caring Deeply about
Church Planting

Caring Deeply about Church Planting

Twelve Keys from the Life of Jesus

Dr. Rich Kao

Routledge
Taylor & Francis Group

A PRODUCTIVITY PRESS BOOK

First published 2021
by Routledge
600 Broken Sound Parkway #300, Boca Raton FL, 33487

and by Routledge
2 Park Square, Milton Park, Abingdon, Oxon, OX14 4RN

Routledge is an imprint of the Taylor & Francis Group, an informa business

Library of Congress Cataloging-in-Publication Data
Names: Kao, Richard, author.
Title: Caring deeply about church planting: twelve keys from the life of Jesus / Dr. Rich Kao, Vancouver, BC.
Description: Boca Raton, FL: Routledge, 2021. | Includes bibliographical references and index. | Summary: "Elite leaders are not just for the arenas of business, politics or the military. They are also to be deployed in the faith sector. None other than Jesus, the founder of Christianity, provides a compelling look at what world-class leadership entails. In this book, twelve keys from the life of Jesus are elucidated which church-planters must keep in mind in order to successfully start new works. Termed Jesus' Model of Impact, these twelve keys follow a three-phase process from conception to construction to disruption. Deeply rooted in Scripture, this book provides guiding principles for church planters working in any culture around the world. Paul's church planting ministry is also highlighted as a powerful confirmation of the keys left to us by Jesus"-- Provided by publisher.
Identifiers: LCCN 2020043196 | ISBN 9780367649999 (pbk) | ISBN 9780367649968 (hbk) | ISBN 9780367649982 (ebk)
Subjects: LCSH: Church development, New. | Christian leadership. | Jesus Christ--Example. | Kao, Richard. Disruptive leadership.
Classification: LCC BV652.24 .K36 2021 | DDC 254/.1--dc23
LC record available at https://lccn.loc.gov/2020043196

ISBN: 9780367649999 (pbk)
ISBN: 9780367649968 (hbk)
ISBN: 9780367649982 (ebk)

Typeset in Minion
by MPS Limited, Dehradun

Contents

Acknowledgments.. vii
About the Author... ix
Introduction: Why I Wrote This Book.. xi

FOUNDATIONS

Chapter 1 Church Planting Is an Organizational Initiative....................3
Chapter 2 Church Planting Is a Breakthrough Initiative.......................7
Chapter 3 Church Planting Is a Prophetic Initiative.......................... 15

PHASE 1—Conception (Leader)

Chapter 4 Key #1—Caring Deeply: The Call of God 25
Chapter 5 Key #2—Clarity: Caring Deeply Must Have a
Compelling, Tangible Goal 29
Chapter 6 Key #3—Capability: Planting Must Be Connected
to Skill, Especially Preaching...................................... 33
Chapter 7 Key #4—Consecration: The Key to Your Plant................. 41

PHASE 2—Construction (New Plant)

Chapter 8 Key #5—Core Team: Finding Those Who Will Plant
with Me.. 49
Chapter 9 Key #6—Culture: How Will This Plant Work, Look,
and Feel?... 57
Chapter 10 Key #7—Creativity: Planting with Genius 67
Chapter 11 Key #8—Coordination: Infrastructure for This Plant 75

PHASE 3—Disruption (Global Impact)

Chapter 12 Key #9—Commitment: Getting the Job Done................. 81

Chapter 13 Key #10—Coin: Faith for Finances 87
Chapter 14 Key #11—Constancy: Protecting the Plant from
Diversions 95
Chapter 15 Key #12—Continuation: Raising Up the New
Disruptors 103

CONCLUSION

Chapter 16 Canvas: Jesus' Model of Impact—Church
Unleashed 111
Chapter 17 Challenge: Paul, Apostle of Love 115
Chapter 18 Coda: God's Glory Rests on the Church 117

MINI-BOOK

Five Stones Church: Our Start-Up Story and a Little Beyond 119

References 159

Index 163

Acknowledgments

This book is the result of a wonderful journey in God, marked by many important people in my life.

First, I want to acknowledge two of my mentors through the years, Jim McCracken and Chuck Porta, who helped to establish, equip, and shape me as a minister. Of note, Chuck's insights into the life of Paul were invaluable in the formulation of my thoughts in this book.

Second, I must acknowledge the key prayer supporters in my life; without their fervent and faithful prayers, who knows where I'd be. A deep heartfelt thanks to Barb, Marion, Pam, Mae, Kim, Diane, Dave, Dick, Pat, Joanne, Paul, George, and the committed ones at Five Stones Church. You are my heroes.

Third, a huge thanks to my wife, Memie, and my four adult children, Kimmie, Heidi, Holly, and Matt. You have helped me in more ways than I could have ever imagined. Your camaraderie, love, support, and understanding in the adventure of planting has been one of the greatest joys of my life.

Last, I'm beyond privileged to be called into the ministry. To Him belongs all the praise.

About the Author

Rich Kao has been in pastoral and church planting ministry for twenty-nine years. He was Senior Pastor of City Hill Fellowship in Minneapolis, Minnesota, before founding Five Stones Church in Vancouver, British Columbia.

Rich has been involved in a variety of start-ups, humanitarian ventures, leadership organizations, and business concerns. He is a member of the Cabinet of Canadians, and has served the Harper Administration and presently the Trudeau Administration on issues of religious freedom and human rights.

Rich also leads the Gospel Cities Initiative, which focuses on planting churches in global cities around the world. He is a frequent conference speaker in Asia.

Prior to being in ministry, Rich worked in the diagnostic and pharmaceutical industries, holding research positions at Kallestad Labs (Hoffman-La Roche) and 3M Co. He is currently a Director with Measurement Technology Laboratories in Minneapolis, Minnesota, a high-tech company specializing in air quality measurement.

He is also Founder and President of a new green company, Hive.City, a design studio that specializes in green event architecture, retail elements, and custom branding by utilizing repurposed paperboard.

He has a BA in biology from Carleton College, an MS in immunology from the University of Minnesota, and a doctorate in strategic leadership (D.SL) from Regent University.

Introduction: Why I Wrote This Book

Never has the need for church planting been more acute or more necessary. The world around us is beset with problems of every kind—political, social, economic, racial, moral. The list is endless, and the difficulties are systemic and entrenched. The best minds, best institutions, and best efforts are being marshaled to address these problems, but are we getting to the root issues? Could it be that the solutions lie elsewhere? Could it be that the problems are spiritual in nature and not just human?

Indeed, the greatest reformer to ever live told us the hope we need comes from the church. Yes, the church, as anemic and as irrelevant as it may seem to some (or many). Jesus said of the community He would birth, "You are the light of the world and the salt of the earth" (Matt. 5:13-14). The church, in all its forms, from small to big, whether found in the countryside or in megacities is God's redeeming force for society, for culture, and for the nations. The church is God's secret weapon and His change agent for the world. He's all in on the church.

As such the church is God's organizational servant in the earth. It's to be an enterprise of the highest quality. It's to sparkle with kingdom power, love, and truth. As Ephesians 3:10 states, "[God's] intent was that now, *through the church*, the manifold wisdom of God should be made known to the rulers and authorities in the heavenly realms."

For such a task outstanding leaders are needed. Great leaders are not just for the arenas of business, politics, or the military. The church must also focus on recruiting, training, and deploying the best. As the leader goes, so goes the organization.

This book is thus written to assist in the great endeavor of planting churches. It's meant to give church planters a biblical and conceptual framework so they can be armed with a map for how to go about establishing new works. This framework is rooted in the humble yet glorious, gentle yet revolutionary ways of Jesus.

Jesus was the best organizational leader to ever live. He came not only to do what the Father told Him to do, but to also give us a universal model we can follow in establishing churches. The fact that thousands of books and articles have been written on this topic bear testimony to the depth of revelation Jesus left for us to mine. This book is humbly offered as another ray of light to that body of work.

My contribution here is to think about church planting in terms of organizational effectiveness, relate it to high-performing leaders, and build it around the core idea of caring deeply. As we will see, it's an integrated model given to us by how Jesus lived and ministered. In modern terms, we could say God has given us a vintage strategy. Vintage-designed things like cars, buildings, and apparel are celebrated and loved for their timeless beauty and usefulness. They are always "in." So it is with the organizational principles we're going to explore; they are vintage because they represent God's enduring pattern regarding the New Testament church. Hence, as we apply them in the twenty-first century, we do so with the same verve and excitement as in the first century. We do this because they are imbued with God's divine insight and understanding.

Part of the model advocated here includes the word "disruption." As a point of definition, disruption is not used in the negative sense in this book. While the word is commonly associated with things like "bad classroom behavior, unruly customers, protestors, or riots" (Kao, 2018, p. xv); disruption in our context is taken as a force for good, like police breaking up a drug bust or a doctor intervening to stop cancer. Disruption here is positive, strong, and transformational.

Jesus was the greatest disruptor to ever live. First, John 3:8 says that Jesus came "to destroy the works of the devil." He disrupted the power of sin and shame. He disrupted people's lives. He disrupted the religious powers of the day. He disrupted cities. He disrupted his own nation. Jesus was the ultimate disruptive leader. And most importantly, His death on the cross was the greatest disruptive event in history. Church planters live in that same vein.

***

This book is actually the book behind the book I recently released for the Silicon Valley crowd, entitled *Disruptive Leadership—Apple and the*

Technology of Caring Deeply: Nine Keys to Organizational Excellence and Global Impact (Kao 2018). It serves as a companion to this book, but this work represents the thoughts and concepts upon which that book was based. This book came first, but it was published second. This book is the "original article."

My prayer is you'll be inspired from the biblical framework presented here and come away better equipped to carry out the incredible call of planting churches to the glory of God.

Dr. Rich Kao
Founding and Sr. Pastor
Five Stones Church
Vancouver, British Columbia

Foundations

1

Church Planting Is an Organizational Initiative

IT ALL BEGINS WITH JESUS

There has never been an organization like it. Over two thousand years ago, with no money and just twelve men, Jesus started the church that has now become, with 2.2 billion people, the largest organization in the world (Pew, 2011). Through persecution, darkness, tribulation, and innumerable attempts to extinguish it, the church has continued to thrive (Broadbent, 1989; Shelley, 1982). How did this happen? How did Jesus accomplish this? As it turns out, much can be learned when we peer into Jesus' remarkable leadership.

THE JESUS MODEL OF IMPACT

Jesus' death on the cross was so consequential that human history is now divided by BC and AD. What Jesus did at Calvary was more significant than man walking on the moon, the harnessing of electricity, or the eradication of polio. It is in a category of its own. How did Jesus, with the subsequent propagation of the good news, come by this historic impact?

Tracing His life, we can see that it first began in the personal arena. His hidden life of thirty years, overflowing with fellowship and communion with God, was preparing him for the historic task ahead (Luke 2:49). Next, it progressed to the organizational arena when he recruited the leaders that would establish the church to disseminate the message of God's salvation (Dever, 2012; Ladd, 1997). Lastly, it would move to a global arena as the gospel would act to transform nations and cultures

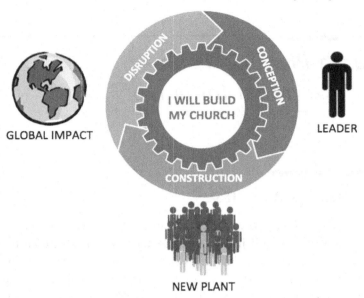

FIGURE 1.1
Jesus' Tri-Phasic Model of Impact

around the world (Mangalwadi, 2009). Taken together, Jesus left us with a model of impact. It begins with conception (leader), progresses to construction (new plant), and ends in disruption (global impact). This model is represented in Figure 1.1.

TWELVE KEYS OF JESUS' MODEL OF IMPACT

This tri-phasic model can be further broken down into twelve keys derived from Jesus' life as the Church's first planter. These keys spring from the core of a leader who cared deeply and sacrificially. There can be no remarkable display of leadership, no excellence in organizational creation, and no global impact without a strongly held, deeply abiding conviction of care. It is central for all the other parts of the model, for from that caring comes the attributes needed to lead, build, and disrupt.

PHASE 1—CONCEPTION (LEADER)

Key #1 Caring Deeply: The Call of God
Key #2 Clarity: Caring Deeply Must Have a Compelling, Tangible Goal
Key #3 Capability: Planting Must Be Connected to Skill, Especially Preaching
Key #4 Consecration: The Key to Your Plant

PHASE 2—CONSTRUCTION (NEW PLANT)

Key #5 Core Team: Finding Those Who Will Plant with Me
Key #6 Culture: How Will This Plant Work, Look, and Feel?
Key #7 Creativity: Planting with Genius
Key #8 Coordination: Infrastructure for This Plant

PHASE 3—DISRUPTION (GLOBAL IMPACT)

Key #9 Commitment: Getting the Job Done
Key #10 Coin: Faith for Finances
Key #11 Constancy: Protecting the Plant from Diversions
Key #12 Continuation: Raising Up the New Disruptors

LIFE OF PAUL

To amplify Jesus' Model of Impact, Paul's signature body of work as an apostle will be profiled. His methods, as given in Acts specifically and the New Testament more broadly, are sine qua non and "can be employed in planting churches in any receptive area of the world" (Ugo, 2012, p. 2). Paul's approach to church planting has global appeal and "envisages a comprehensive idea." He possessed "an inventive personality [that] used innovative methods to reach people" (Johnson, n.d., p. 27). The principles of Pauline planting, not surprisingly, track elegantly with Jesus' Model of Impact.

When Jesus said, "I will build my church and the gates of hell will not prevail" (Matt. 16:18), Paul took that mandate to heart and ran with it with all his might—through imprisonments, beatings, lashings, dangers, hardships, hunger, and more (1 Cor. 11:23–27). Jesus provided the foundation upon which to plant churches, and Paul became its premier practitioner. As expressed in the academic literature and in popular articles, Paul is celebrated as one of the greatest pioneering church planters of all time. The inclusion of Paul's ministry in this book serves as a study within a study.

But before we begin this journey, we need to look at other two foundational truths underpinning the activity of church planting: (1) it is a breakthrough initiative, and (2) it is a prophetic initiative.

2

Church Planting Is a Breakthrough Initiative

One of the most compelling stories related to church planting begins in the Old Testament. When David defeated Goliath, this was not just a great Sunday school story or a powerful biographical moment in David's life, it represented something more. David embodied the heart and spirit of what is required in a planter. His improbable victory over the giant represented a breakthrough spirit that God imparts to all who are called to start a new work. David's conquest was a victory for the ages, yet within his story is a powerful picture of what it means to be a breakthrough leader. It helps to define what the assignment of church planting is all about.

DAVID TAKES OUT GOLIATH

David's job was to simply bring food to his brothers on the front lines of the battlefield (1 Sam. 17:17-18). Tasked by his father to bring grain, bread, and cheese, he could have never imagined how his small assignment would lead to a pivotal turning point in the nation.

As Saul's army was conducting their morning exercises, Goliath, the champion of the Philistines would issue his daily taunts against the soldiers. "I defy the ranks of Israel this day; give me a man that we may fight together" (1 Sam. 17:10). Saul would grant a prize—his daughter in marriage and great riches—to any man that would fight the giant (1 Sam. 17:25). But no man responded, until David.

David was incredulous to hear such a challenge. "Who is this uncircumcised Philistine, that he should taunt the armies of the living God?" (1 Sam. 17:26). David was provoked and his question was not merely rhetorical; it expressed his intent to enter the fray. No enemy should speak like that of God's people. David would not allow such impunity to go unchecked. Having honed his slinging skills in defense of the flock, he could kill marauding lions or bears with deadly accuracy. Goliath would be no different, save that he was an even bigger target to hit. David's innate sense of indignation took over. No spirit of intimidation would rule Israel. He would act.

Thus began one of the greatest personal acts of valor in military history. Without hesitation, David ran quickly toward Goliath and, with a solo shot from his sling, felled the giant. David seized the giant's sword and proceeded to cut off Goliath's head. Just like that the battle was over (1 Sam. 17:48-51). The Philistines, seeing their champion vanquished, fled en masse. The sons of Israel quickly followed with a great plundering of the enemy's camps (1 Sam. 17:52-53). The rout was on. Breakthrough had come.

Just as David's victory represented the heart and pluck required to take out age-old enemies and open up new territories, so it is with church planting. Philistine attitudes loom large. Its shadow casts a pall of heaviness over all who are near. Intimidation, disdain, and outright hostility can await new works. Yet, David's story provides an inspiring view of how when one is called by God, even the most difficult of problems can be defeated. Out with the old and in with the new. Disruption is at hand.

THE PROTOTYPE BREAKTHROUGH LEADER

David's victory did not happen by chance. His victory was not because of a lucky shot, like a half-court basket made by a random student picked out of the stands. On the contrary, everything about David's life, though only a young man at the time, paints a vivid picture of what it takes to be a breakthrough leader.

Cultivate a Continuous Secret History with God (1 Sam. 16:11)

Before there can be any external victory, there must be inner dealings and a secret history with God. David nurtured a hidden life. He embraced his anonymity as the eighth son, forgotten among his brothers, as he tended sheep in the fields.

God's promotion came to David not on the basis of visibility or no-
toriety, it came on the basis of what was in his heart (1 Sam. 16:7). God
delights in fellowship. He sees our prayers, adoration, and worship. He
sees the small acts of obedience and unannounced commitments to
consecration and sanctification. He sees the wrestling over sins and the
desire to become a godly vessel.

Jeremiah 9:23-24: "Thus says the LORD, 'Let not a wise man boast of his
wisdom, and let not the mighty man boast of his might, let not a rich
man boast of his riches; but let him who boasts boast of this, that he
understands and knows Me.'"

John 17:3: "This is eternal life, that they may know You, the only true
God, and Jesus Christ whom You have sent."

Philippians 3:8, 14: "More than that, I count all things to be loss in view
of the surpassing value of knowing Christ Jesus. ... I press on toward
the goal for the prize of the upward call of God in Christ Jesus."

Build Your Leadership Résumé (1 Sam. 17:36)

Are there conquests of lions and bears on your résumé as David had? If
you want people to follow you, there had better be a reason to do so. If
you're an emerging leader, don't rush to the number-one slot. Get some
wins. Prove yourself. Don't try to be the lead guy until you've got something to show for it. King Saul, who preceded David, had no wins on his
résumé. The people had to follow him because of his position. This was
not ideal. Instead, be a leader that people want to follow. Therefore, be
intentional and faithful in building your leadership credibility.

Play Offense: See Giants as Opportunities, Not Threats (1 Sam. 17:48)

A by-product of cultivating intimacy with God and building our leadership skills is that dominion grows inside of us. A boldness and
courage becomes part of our personality. We don't have to strive for it; it
becomes part of who we are. We become first movers. We play offense.
1 Samuel 17:48 says, "David *ran* quickly toward the battle line." We don't
retreat from Goliaths in fear. Rather, we see giants as an opportunity.

Malcolm Gladwell, in his book *David and Goliath*, makes an interesting case about the giant. He says researchers conjecture that Goliath

suffered from a medical condition called acromegaly, in which the pituitary gland overproduces human growth hormone due to the presence of a benign tumor acting on the gland. Not only do those with acromegaly grow abnormally tall and big, but their vision is also affected, due to pressure on their optic nerves; this leads to blurred and double vision. The medical experts suggest Goliath had this condition because when he saw David with his shepherd's rod, he said, "Why are you coming to me with sticks"—plural (1 Sam. 17:43). As big and foreboding as Goliath was, in fact, he may have had a vision problem, which may have explained why he had an attendant (1 Sam. 17:51); the armor-bearer would lead him to where he needed to stand in battle.

It's an interesting hypothesis. But whether Gladwell is right about Goliath's medical condition or not, this we know: Goliath's threat was overstated as David took him out with a savviness the giant did not expect.

Clearly there are giants in the land today: cynicism, intellectualism, materialism, greed, hedonism, indifference, disdain, unbelief, broken homes, divorces, sexual abuse, addictions, and more. If we gaze upon the Goliaths, it's easy to feel overwhelmed. But if our gaze is upon the Lord, we will have boldness and a mind to go on the offense.

Gladwell does well to describe David as a projectile warrior, whereas Goliath was an infantryman—versed in armor, sword, and shields but no match for David's speed and maneuverability. Goliath was a ground man; David was an airman. Because of this, David changed the terms of engagement.

Is this not what Jesus taught: if they hit you, turn the other cheek; if they ask you to go one mile, go two? If they persecute you, pray for your enemies and love them (Matt. 5:38-46). How can the world cope with such weapons? This is the way of the gospel. Can anything overcome it? In every generation, God is looking to mobilize those who will prove the power of the gospel. The gospel is for all ages, for all times. The gospel overcomes all.

Own Your Way of Winning. You Have a Sling (1 Sam. 17:40)

David's weapon of victory was his sling, not Saul's gear. We all have been given a way of winning by God. While it may be tempting to suit up with someone's armor, that is not our best choice. If you're good at praying, win with it. If you're good at counseling, win with it. If you excel at mercy, win with it. If you're good at organizing, win with it. That's your sling. Don't compare yourself to anyone else. God gave it to you to win the war.

David didn't try to be like Saul's soldiers. He had not learned Saul's way of warfare. David was "outside the system." David was trained in the fields of Bethlehem. His boot camp was the frigid nights and blazing hot days of the pasturelands. While Saul's men were learning about spears and javelins and sizing their helmets, David was working on his aim from thirty yards. Every one of us has been schooled by God in a special way. There are no experiences, painful or otherwise, that go to waste. Every single one of us has a genuine leather, custom-fitted sling that has our name etched on it. That sling is our implement of victory.

Take Dead Aim at the Head (1 Sam. 17:51)

Why is there so much antipathy toward the gospel? Because Philistine thinking lives inside the thoughts of people. David did not kill Goliath with an arrow to the heart, rather he was felled by a stone to the head. The mind is where the strongholds are.

Never have our pulpits been more important. We are called to preach with passion and clarity. Jesus wasn't killed for His good works, walking on water, or raising people from the dead. Jesus was killed for what He preached, because the truth under the Holy Spirit's anointing takes dead aim at people's thinking.

For someone to come to faith in Jesus Christ, their thinking must first be challenged. The word *repentance* means to change one's mind. That is no small battle. Gospel truths are like smooth stones flying toward its listener with drone like accuracy. It has penetrating power and acts to undo thinking that keeps people from experiencing God.

Know Your Culture: Be Creative (1 Sam. 17:43)

When David went to engage Goliath, the giant was insulted by the young foe standing in front of him, "What is this dog you're sending out against me?" (1 Sam. 17:43). He was completely caught off guard. Herein lies a powerful lesson. The world has one picture of the church but God has a new presentation, one that catches the world by surprise. The gospel never changes, but the "delivery systems" do. This speaks to the church's invitation to harness creativity and innovation in doing kingdom work; to deploy fresh strategies ("David's") that causes the current culture to do a "double take." God loves to equip planters with new technologies that causes the world to get a fresh view of the church, and creativity is a key in that process.

There is an additional point to note. Before David deployed his new sling technology, he first honored Saul; he tried on the King's armor (1 Sam. 17:38). This tells us that while we may have new technologies in our pockets that shift away from old paradigms, we shouldn't deploy them without honoring the past. A disruptive leader is not a disrespectful leader. He or she pivots from the old to the new with the blessing of the previous government whenever he can.

The Lord's Name Is Your Main Thing (1 Sam. 17:45)

Creativity must be wedded to the Spirit's anointing. When David went to war, he said, "I come to you in the name of the Lord of hosts." When all is said and done, nothing replaces the power of the Holy Spirit. The third person of the Trinity is not negotiable. We can't slay giants in the name of ourselves or our own strength. It's the Spirit who gives life, the flesh profits nothing (John 6:63). If we are unsure of our conviction on this, the Enemy will use it to exploit our double-mindedness to erode our impact and effectiveness.

Have Thick Skin

New initiatives are always associated with a certain amount of cow pie. Eliab, David's oldest brother said, "Why have you come down? I know your insolence" (1 Sam. 17:28). People will question what we're doing, our motivation, our qualifications, our intent— even those close to us. We need to have thick skin. We can't let the naysayers keep us out of the fray. We'll have to weather criticism and misunderstanding. Keep your eye on the prize. Hold on to the clarity and determination God has given you.

Love the People, and They Will Love You Back

David was a man of the sheep, sacrificially taking care of them day and night (1 Sam. 17:34-35). This is how the people come around us, rally to us, and go to war with us. If you love them, they will love you back (most of the time). And when they love you back, you have people you can shape to be influencers.

In all this, David displayed the ways of a breakthrough leader. Church planters will do themselves well to keep this example regularly in mind as they take on their big assignments from God.

3

Church Planting Is a Prophetic Initiative

ANTIOCH: THE NEW REFERENCE POINT

Whereas Jerusalem anchored the first twelve chapters of Acts, the scene switches at the halfway point in the book. In chapter 13, Antioch emerges as the new epicenter of apostolic activity.

Having begun in Acts 11 as a small outpost of Gentile evangelism, Antioch would soon become the main engine of the gospel. While Peter and his compatriots had set the pace in the opening frame at Pentecost, soon a new leadership team would emerge to power forward the advancement of the good news to the "uttermost parts of the earth" (Acts 1:8). Not only would the gospel claim new territories and beachheads, but the activity and habits of the Antioch leaders would set a new tone.

Humble and hidden from view, the five core leaders of the Antioch church came together to pray and fast (Acts 13:2). Like the Jerusalem apostles before them, they "devoted themselves to the ministry of the word and prayer" (Acts 6:4). It was a multicultural, multiethnic team, made up of a black man (Niger), a Roman (Lucius), a Hebrew biblical scholar (Paul), a politically connected man (Manaen), and Barnabas who served as their team leader (Acts 13:1). It couldn't have been more diverse, and yet it couldn't have represented God's future intentions more perfectly. The gospel would be borne by believers from every nation, every socioeconomic strata, and every corner of life. It would be the good news for all peoples.

As the team was "ministering to the Lord" (Acts 13:2), the Holy Spirit moved in their midst and released a bold word: send out a new church planting team. But this would not be just any church planting team; it would be one made up of the founders. Though the Antioch church was still young, the Holy Spirit directed to send out the top leaders. Barnabas and Paul would be "set apart for the work to which I have called them" (Acts 13:2). In effect, the Holy Spirit was saying, "Don't hold back. Send out the best." Yes, it would radically change the leadership equation at home, but the gospel was on the move. There was no time to lose. And as the saying goes, the rest is history. But, in this pivotal scene, we are not only given a riveting look at what transpired in that leadership meeting, we are also taught how church planting is a prophetic initiative.

First, this moment served to codify one of the highest principles of church planting. It must be initiated by God in heaven. *Disruption begins before the throne*—in worship, in prayer, in intercession, and in delighting in God. This is the prelude to all missional activity: "Not by might, not by power, but by my Spirit says the Lord" (Zech. 4:6). This was a prophetic moment of huge proportions, although when experienced in real time by the team, they probably had no idea what was to unfold.

Second, church planting is a leadership intensive enterprise. As the head flows, so flows the body. Starting new works requires the best leadership the church can offer. That the Holy Spirit dispatched the two top leaders of the church was a radical move, to say the least—and in many ways, counterintuitive. Wasn't the newly formed congregation too young to stand on its own? Didn't they need more shepherding and guidance? Were they really trained enough to carry on the work? No, this was not a premature move. The Holy Spirit had all things in hand. Both the home base and the new planting team would do well. The tip of the spear had to possess the sharpest point, and Barnabas and Paul were no doubt the sharpest, most gifted men that could be commissioned.

Third, the pairing of Paul and Barnabas represents the biblical priority of having apostles and prophets work in tandem. Later, Paul would write that the church is built on the "foundation of the apostles and prophets, Christ Jesus Himself being the cornerstone" (Eph. 2:20). Paul would even go on to assign a rank to these offices. "God has appointed in the church, first apostles, second prophets" (1 Cor. 12:28). Something magical and potent happens when apostles and prophets work together to bring their visionary, dynamic, forward-moving, faith-challenging, mountain-taking, flag-planting, over–the–river-and-through-the-woods, and Jesus-glorifying ways. They represent a dynamic duo.

Fourth, church planting is entrepreneurial by nature. It's a start-up gig. Pioneering and establishing require risk-takers. It requires those who can deal with uncertainty and shifting scenarios. Those who start with the plant may not continue with the plant. Personnel changes. Finances are unpredictable. Strategies fail. Disappointments can abound. The circle of safety is small. There are no comfortable offices, reliable paychecks, or dependable staff. Church planters must be polymaths, or at least be ready to do anything and everything that's needed—and sometimes all at the same time.

Fifth, church planting requires a deep dependence on the person of the Holy Spirit. No doubt there were times when Paul and Barnabas wondered if they were doing the right thing. No doubt they had their moments of wanting to retreat and shrink back. But the voice of the Holy Spirit was so clear when the five leaders had come together to pray. That moment was their faith anchor. They were not there by accident. This was not their own doing or idea. They were appointed for this work. Without the guidance and assurance of the Holy Spirit, no one can or should take on the insanity of starting a new work. It's too hard. It can be heartbreaking. Yet it's the Holy Spirit who changes everything. His guidance and comfort provide the grace needed to do the uncommon. He's the super in supernatural.

Sixth, church planting targets key cities. More on this later, but when one studies the progression of Paul's three missionary tours, we see the distinct strategy of reaching key cities. As Tim Keller (2010, p. 130) has written, "In Acts 17, Paul goes to Athens, the intellectual center of the Greco-Roman world, and then in Acts 18 to Corinth, one of the commercial centers of the empire, and then in Acts 19 to Ephesus, often seen as the religious center of the Roman world. Paul by the end of Acts makes it to Rome, which was the military and political center of that world. In his commentary on the book of Acts, John Stott concludes, 'It seems to have been Paul's deliberate policy to move purposefully from one strategic city-centre to the next.'"

Seventh, given the city-centric strategy of Paul, church planting requires crossing ethnic boundaries and becoming cross-culturally agile. Just as Jesus left heaven to come to earth, requiring Him to radically adapt to new environments, so planting in new cities and new countries, among new people, requires adaptation. Provincialism won't cut it. Church planters need a global mindset. One must be able to embrace new foods, new ways of dressing, new smells, new systems, new customs, new ways of relating, new languages, new value systems, and new ways of communicating. It's not easy, and many times it's not fun. But the effort to appreciate, respect, and enjoy new cultures is a key to reaching the people.

Eighth, church planting lives off supernatural financial provision. Church planters must have faith in this area. One of the ongoing miracles of establishing new churches is how God provides financially. Time and again, we see this is one of God's most concrete ways of encouraging the planter. When there are only drops of oil left in the jar, God comes to sustain the supply (1 Kings 17:8-16). When money is needed to pay one's taxes, the coin is in the fish's mouth (Matt. 17:24-27). When the crowds need to be fed, the bread will be multiplied (Matt. 14:13-21). When Paul needed assistance to continue his work, the Philippians sent him aid (Phil. 1:3-5; 4:15-18). Jesus supported the twelve disciples and their families. Paul worked with his hands, making tents when necessary (Acts 18:3). By any and all means, planters stretch a dollar and believe for the bank account to be filled. Modern support-raising methods are great, but in the end, provision for the work is powered by trust in God.

Ninth, church planting is a multiplicative ministry. New disciples. New planters. New works. It all goes back to the Great Commission: "Go therefore and make disciples of all nations" (Matt. 28:19). This is how the kingdom expands. The kingdom DNA is transferred person-to-person, leader-to-leader, and church-to-church. It begins before the throne and it ends in multiplication. That's the prophetic agenda and God's divine strategy.

SMALL IS BIG

Having established the prophetic ethos of church planting, we can look at this from another angle. Paul's ways are a picture of the adage "Small Is Big," or to borrow a popular business term, Paul established the "Biblical Lean Model" of kingdom advancement.

When I refer to "Small Is Big," I'm referring to a seminal blog entry posted by well-known *Purple Cow* author Seth Godin. In that post, he was flying the flag of Pauline church planting without knowing it. I post key segments of his entry here:

Seth Godin—June 5, 2005—Small Is Big

Big used to matter.

Big planes were better than small ones, because they were faster and more efficient. Big buildings were better than small ones because they facilitated communications and used downtown land quite efficiently. Bigger computers could handle more simultaneous users, as well.

Get Big Fast was the motto for startups, because big companies can go public and get more access to capital and use that capital to get even bigger. Big accounting firms were the place to go to get audited if you were a big company, because a big accounting firm could be trusted. Big law firms were the place to find the right lawyer, because big law firms were a one-stop shop.

And then small happened.

Enron (big) got audited by Andersen (big) and failed (big.) The World Trade Center was a target. TV advertising is collapsing so fast you can hear it. American Airlines (big) is getting creamed by Jet Blue (think small). Boing Boing (four people) has a readership growing a hundred times faster than the New Yorker (hundreds of people).

Today, little companies often make more money than big companies. Little churches grow faster than worldwide ones. Little jets are way faster (door to door) than big ones.

Today, Craigslist (18 employees) is the fourth most visited site according to some measures. They are partly owned by eBay (more than 4,000 employees) which hopes to stay in the same league, traffic-wise. They're certainly not growing nearly as fast.

Small is the new big because small gives you the flexibility to change the business model when your competition changes theirs.

Is it better to be the head of Craigslist or the head of UPS?

Small is the new big only when the person running the small thinks big. Don't wait. Get small. Think big.

***

Bravo Seth. This is what we call a "biblical-echo" piece—giving voice to a biblical principle in a nonreligious context. In Seth's case, he's talking about the power of small in business. In actuality, he took a page right out of Paul's playbook.

Think about how Paul started churches:

- No big overhead (but nothing wrong with overhead).
- No big staff (but nothing wrong with large staff).

- No big buildings (but nothing wrong with nice buildings).
- No big purse (but nothing wrong with having lots of money).
- No big fundraising campaign (but nothing wrong with support raising).
- No big advertising budget (but nothing wrong with getting the word out).
- No big ramp-up campaign (but nothing wrong with prelaunch strategies).

Paul was lean and mean. He was nimble, flexible, and able to pivot quickly (e.g., Acts 16:7-10). He was able to do a lot with a little. Simplicity was his friend. He was the ultimate bootstrapper. But let's not confuse "small" with small outcomes. Paul planted high-impact churches because of what God had deposited inside of him.

- Big heart
- Big vision
- Big determination
- Big love for culture
- Big Bible expertise
- Big heart for people
- Big anointing
- Big calling
- Big prayer life

It's all about the DNA.

Does this not reflect the mustard seed and yeast teachings Jesus gave us about the church? Indeed, they are. The mustard seed is the smallest of seeds, yet "when it is full grown, it is larger than the garden plants, and becomes a tree, so that the birds of the air come and nest in its branches" (Matt. 13:32). The yeast is hidden in the flour but makes the entire dough to rise—sixty pounds of it (Matt. 13:33). Yeast cells can only be seen under the microscope, yet it produces tens of pounds of bread in one production run, enough to feed a small army (Matt. 13:33). Small is not just big, it's huge! That's how God designed it. His delight is to take insignificant, small, unseen, cast-aside, unnoticed, weak, unsuspecting things and turn them into something great (1 Cor. 1:26-28). Think the two spies—unnamed (Josh. 2:1). Think Gideon—full of fear (Judg. 6:11).

Think Mary—teenage mom (Luke 1:26-38). Think the widow's mite—sacrificial giving (Mark 12:42). It's how God rolls.

***

Having established the breakthrough and prophetic nature of church planting, we now turn back to the organizational strategy given to us by Jesus, and the care-inspired progression from conception to construction to disruption.

Phase I

Conception (Leader)

4

Key #1 — Caring Deeply: The Call of God

"I must be about my Father's business" (Luke 2:49).

Every great leader has a vision to change the world, "to put a dent in the universe" (Snell, 2011). Jesus was the ultimate world changer. Scriptures tell us that in view of humanity's sin, God sent His only begotten Son into this world to redeem it. Jesus lived to die. There is no higher expression of caring than that. At the center of His being was an ocean of love for humanity (John 3:16; 1 John 4:8). In the depths of His heart was a vision to save man from his predicament and a burden that none would perish (1 Tim. 2:4; 1 Peter 3:18; 2 Peter 3:9). Care would be His fuel to do supernatural deeds and demonstrate world-class leadership. It was the fountainhead from which everything else would flow.

How does God develop care in our lives? How does He move and deepen our love for people? By taking us through the peaks and valleys of life. Jesus lost his father at a young age, and, as the oldest in the family, likely had to assume responsibility for the home. Taking over his father's carpentry shop, Jesus had the burden of running the business and providing for the family. He had to be a listening ear to his mother, pray for a flow of customers to keep income coming in, and be a fatherly figure to his siblings. He could have easily fallen to the side of resentment and bitterness, seeing as how many of his friends and peers didn't have to shoulder what He did; but instead, He used the situation to understand the grit of life in which people lived. His sympathy grew deeply as He came to understand the aspirations and hopes of people around him. Jesus would show unfailing kindness to all, but a stark reality would always loom; there would be no whitewashing of the sin constantly at work in people's lives. It was the ugly underbelly in every situation.

Each and every day the dysfunction could be seen in His own small village of Nazareth. Every day He could see the effects of human beings' fallen nature—their greed, their anger, their rage, their lust, their covetousness, their selfishness. He could see it in His siblings and His mother. The condition of humanity was intractable. No matter how much they tried, they couldn't improve themselves. Yes, there could be incremental gains, but no fundamental ones.

And therein lay Jesus' mission. His conversations and meditations, the study of the Scriptures, and fellowship with His heavenly Father began to take on experiential weight. He would begin to apprehend the everlasting love the Father had for the world. Jesus would begin to assimilate the very heart the Father had for humanity. As God began to reveal Jesus' unique birth and His divine nature, Jesus would discern the call God was putting upon Him. He was to give His life for the sins of the world. This was not a mission of obligation. It would be a mission of love. No man would deter Him from going to the cross. He would weather difficulties and misunderstandings, even from His own family. He would have to challenge the very traditions of His people and their understanding of the Law. Faith would save the people, not works.

The Father would endow Jesus with unparalleled power from the Holy Spirit to express His heart for the multitudes trapped in sickness, heaviness, bondage, and hopelessness. Jesus would work miracles, but all in service of His ultimate call—to give His life for the sins of the world. He would die a humiliating death, not because raging forces inexplicably overtook His life, but because they were sovereignly orchestrated by His all-knowing Father, down to the donkey upon which He would ride into Jerusalem. Jesus endured it all because He cared. For the joy set before Him, He endured the cross, despising the shame, and sat down at the right hand of the throne of God (Heb. 12:2). **Care changes the world.**

PAUL: APPREHENDED FOR CHRIST

"I did not prove disobedient to the heavenly vision" (Acts 26:19).

While journeying on the road to Damascus, Paul had a life-altering encounter with the risen Christ. Prior to this, Paul was deeply committed to "being hostile, locking up the saints, punishing them often in all synagogues, forcing them to blaspheme, and being furiously enraged at them" (Acts 26:9-11).

But all that changed when Jesus shone upon the chief persecutor at midday, "brighter than the sun" (Acts 26:13). Jesus' revealing of Himself came with such force that Paul and his companions were knocked to the ground (Acts 26:13-14a). Whereas Jesus was previously a menace to the Jewish people, Paul now addressed Him with a new respect (Acts 26:14).

> [Paul] said, "Who are You, Lord?" And the Lord said, "I am Jesus whom you are persecuting. But get up and stand on your feet; for this purpose I have appeared to you, to appoint you a minister and a witness not only to the things which you have seen, but also to the things in which I will appear to you; rescuing you from the Jewish people and from the Gentiles, to whom I am sending you, to open their eyes so that they may turn from darkness to light and from the dominion of Satan to God, that they may receive forgiveness of sins and an inheritance among those who have been sanctified by faith in Me." (Acts 26:15-18)

Through this encounter, Paul the persecutor became a man with a new heart and a new call. Jesus' apprehending of Paul upended everything in his life, and, as humbling as it was, nothing was dearer to Paul than the day his life was turned around, "So, King Agrippa, I did not prove disobedient to the heavenly vision" (Acts 26:19).

Paul was so radically changed by his Damascus conversion that he would tell the Corinthian church, "Woe is me if I do not preach the gospel" (1 Cor. 9:16). Just as the great prophet Isaiah first uttered "Woe is me" when he saw the Lord high and lifted up (Isa. 6:1-5), so Paul would give voice to that same devastating feeling. When God calls, He touches our innermost being. This is how God prepares His servants to plant churches. Be not surprised that God puts a "woe" inside of you. It's Him putting His care and burden in you to change the world. It's the start of something powerful.

ACTIVATION—CARING DEEPLY (#1)

1. Describe why you care deeply about your call.
2. A remarkable leader is defined as one who cares deeply *and sacrificially* (p. 8). What kind of sacrifice has your call produced in you? Name three examples of how it has played out in your life.
3. What inspires you most from Jesus' or Paul's life about how they cared deeply and sacrificially?
4. What natural things in your life have shaped your call? What events have happened that make you care deeply about what you're going to do?

5

Key #2—Clarity: Caring Deeply Must Have a Compelling, Tangible Goal

"I came to seek and save the lost" (Luke 19:10).

Clarity is related to calling, and is sometimes equated with calling, but here it refers to fine-tuning the call. The rumblings and burdens of caring deeply must eventually be synthesizable and reducible to a crystal-clear idea, a sentence, a memorable phrase, or a one-thought action plan. At first, when God opens our eyes, we see the trees but not perfectly (Mark 8:23-24). We know the field we need to head toward, but we need more insights, more discussions, and more prayer. When Jesus prayed for the blind man *a second time*, the Scriptures say the blind man "looked intently and was restored and began to see everything clearly" (Mark 8:25). Clarity is an iterative exercise. It's process-driven, and it takes time—sometimes years.

Jesus developed crystal-clear vision through years of listening, honing, and getting it right in His spirit. At age twelve, He knew He had to be "in His Father's house" (Luke 2:49). The call was there. But what did that mean? Would He be a teacher? Would He be a rabbi? Would He be a prophet? Yes, these would all be parts of his call but not the main part. Rather, His destiny would be to seek and save the lost (Luke 19:10). The Savior's ministry would be His central purpose. His love for the world had an "executable" and a clear "actionable." Caring deeply moves to reality when it has a clear goal.

Because Jesus understood the power of clarity, he wanted others to have it as well. Thus, He taught, "Seek first the kingdom of God" (Matt. 6:33). He preached about praying and fasting (Matt. 6:5-18). He modeled the necessity of personal seclusion by retreating to mountainsides (Mark 1:35; Matt. 14:23), or "slip[ping] away to the wilderness" (Luke 5:16). He would never allow the demands of ministry to rob him of His need to hear from the Father and remain centered. His disciplines removed any haziness or uncertainty about what He was to do. Everything in His life, in His organization, and for the men around Him would be properly ordered. Seeking God in the service of clarity is a must for every church planter. Clarity is a blessing God loves to give.

PAUL: CALLED TO THE GENTILES

"He is a chosen instrument to bear my Name before the Gentiles" (Acts 9:15).

As told by God at his conversion, Paul's call would be to the Gentiles (Acts 9:15). God had called the original apostles from the shores of Galilee to steward the gospel to the Jewish world, but Paul's ministry would be aimed at the Gentile world. The twelve apostles would focus on Jerusalem, Judea, and Samaria, and Paul would focus on the uttermost parts of the earth. The Twelve would be stationed in Jerusalem, but Paul's ministry would be mobile, traversing the Roman Empire. The Twelve were "uneducated" and from the countryside; Paul was highly educated and from the city. The apostles were primarily monocultural in their upbringing, while Paul was multicultural. God's division of labor was clear. Each one was raised up in just the right way for their respective calls.

Waiting in Clarity for Clarity

Interestingly, it would be twelve years before Paul officially moved into his ministry. He spent this time out of the public eye in Tarsus (Acts 9:30; Gal. 1:17). Why this long wait? Because God had to form the message inside the messenger. This shows us the "what" is as important as the "where." We need as much clarity about what and how to do something as to where to go. To reach the Gentiles, Paul needed a full and complete understanding of the new covenant and the gospel of grace. He would have to understand it from the Old Testament in light of Christ's work on the cross. He would need to know how to defend it, preach it, and how to apply it in the varied situations he would face.

This would not be something he could learn from other people, this had to be divinely imparted to him (Gal. 1:11-12).

He had to understand the overwhelming nature of God's love (Rom. 8:37-39; Eph. 3:16-19); the utter divinity and supremacy of Jesus (Col. 1:15-20); and how Jesus was better in every way—whether it pertained to angels, Moses, Joshua, the Aaronic priesthood, or anything else (Heb. 1-13). He had to fully grasp how propitiation and justification and glorification converged in Christ (Rom. 1-8). He had to understand how the law of the Spirit triumphed over the law of sin and death (Rom. 8:1). He had to come into a revelation of the new creation (2 Cor. 5:17). He had to understand the eschatological implications of Jesus' return (1 Thess. 5; 2 Thess. 2). He had to receive God's wisdom about spiritual gifts, the number of them, the definition of them, and how they were to be used in a congregation (1 Cor. 12-14). He had to see how the prophet-priest-king paradigm in the Old Testament was making way for the new governmental structure of apostle-prophet-evangelist-pastor-teacher (Eph. 4:11). He had to gain insight into sonship and the inheritance that came with being in Christ (Eph. 1:1-14). He had to come into a reworked understanding of natural Israel's ongoing role within the new covenant (Rom. 9-11).

The amount of truth he had to process was mind-blowing. That's why he prayed that the saints would be given a like "spirit of wisdom and revelation in the knowledge of Him … that our hearts would be enlightened, so that we would know what is the hope of His calling, what are the riches of the glory of His inheritance in the saints, and what is the surpassing greatness of His power towards us who believe" (Eph. 1:17-19). In the giving of these truths to Paul, God even took him up "into Paradise and [he] heard inexpressible words which a man is not permitted to speak" (2 Cor. 12:4). But to keep Paul from falling into pride for the "surpassing greatness of the revelations" he was given, Paul was given a thorn in the flesh (2 Cor. 12:7).

The message Paul received to preach to the Gentiles was unprecedented. Like a church bell, it would soon ring beautifully throughout Paul's ministry, calling the nations to Christ. Paul waited in clarity for clarity.

ACTIVATION—CLARITY (#2)

1. Read Mark 8:22–26. Explain where you are in the story. Have you received your first touch or second touch? This first touch is having your eyes opened to where you're supposed to head (you see the field of trees, v. 24). The second touch is high-definition clarity. You see so clearly now, you can walk in your "new vision."

2. When Paul waited in clarity (knowing to whom he was sent) for clarity (what he was to say to them), he was waiting for his "second touch." He knew he was called to the Gentiles, but God needed to give him the message. Sometimes the second touch can take years. How long have you been waiting for the second touch? If you've had your second touch, what testimony or encouragement can you share with others about waiting on God?

6

Key #3 — Capability: Planting Must Be Connected to Skill, Especially Preaching

"The Spirit of the Lord is upon me" (Luke 4:18).

While the motivation to do God's will can be strong, it must be connected to skill. Otherwise, the dream cannot be acted upon. Jesus began growing His skills at a young age, and as the Scripture testifies of his development, "[He] kept increasing in wisdom and stature" (Luke 2:52). He trained his mind, dialogued with the best teachers, and prioritized learning over boyish activities (Luke 2:41-49). Jesus was committed to His craft at an early age.

Though educated outside the mainstream of Jerusalem rabbinical tradition (John 7:14-15), Jesus nevertheless gave Himself to the rigors of elite training and understood the paramount priority of wedding intellect to devotion. The resultant combination of study and worship caused Jesus to be a child prodigy. "All who heard him [at twelve years of age] were amazed at His understanding and answers" (Luke 2:47). The foundation for teaching a nation was being established. Yet His superior wisdom was no grounds for pride. Jesus would steadfastly wait until the right moment when the "Spirit of the Lord would be upon Him" so as to be duly anointed for the task ahead (Luke 4:18).

Part of Jesus' development was, in his humanity, to respect the place of earthly authority in His life. Though beyond His parents in spiritual insight, the Bible says, "He continued in subjection to them" (Luke 2:51). Jesus understood that being in submission was key to cultivating the right spirit. The Father works through authority, whereas the devil works through rebellion. Part of Jesus' skill formation was learning self-control. Leaders want to lead. But that impulse must be placed under the yoke of the Holy Spirit. Learning to be controlled by the Spirit is a key attribute of being a kingdom leader.

NATURAL BECOMES SPIRITUAL

Besides Jesus' spiritual development, God also used Jesus' vocation as a carpenter for His preparation (Mk. 6:3). Many of the underlying habits and skills needed to run the family business would directly transfer to His call. As His earthly father Joseph taught him to build pieces of furniture, there was an apprenticing process Jesus followed that would later cross over to His own mentoring approach. "Knowledge transfer" would occur in the context of everyday life—blending daily routines and work with spiritual teaching. This would not be a "classroom" approach, but a "doing life together" approach (Deut. 6:4-9). And just as Jesus gained much from having His natural father mentor him, so Jesus would mentor His disciples with a father's heart.

Jesus also learned management skills—how to keep the books up to date; scheduling and planning for delivery of goods; providing quality products to build a reputation; customer follow-up; forecasting sales; praying for provision; understanding the value of hard work; and tithing income back to God. All these things contributed to Jesus possessing a responsible and excellent spirit. He was attentive to detail, a craftsman, at ease with clients, sympathetic, a problem-solver, and a man with a good name. These early years would later lead to big things.

God wastes nothing. No matter what path a planter takes, whether through seminary or the marketplace, they are all "schools" in God's hands. They are part of His formation process to make sure the planter is properly equipped, because the people led by him or her will depend on it. One's credibility depends in part on one's capabilities. Followers must see competency and skill in their leaders in order to follow.

PREACHING IS PRIME

While the list of Jesus' capabilities is many, there is one that sits at the top of them all, and it's the most important one for the planter: the ability to preach. When the multitudes heard Jesus speak, they exclaimed, "Where did this man get His wisdom?" (Matt. 13:54). "The multitudes were amazed at His teaching, for His message was with authority" (Luke 4:32; Matt. 7:28). "The great throng heard Him gladly" (Mark 12:37). "Never did a man speak the way this man speaks" (John 7:46). "To whom shall we go? You have the words of eternal life" (John 6:68).

There can be no planting unless there is a man who can preach. One of the unique ways in which God establishes His kingdom is through the medium of speaking. It's His way of communicating and establishing authority upon which a church must be built. We see this at the Bible's outset. "In the beginning, God *said...*" (Gen. 1:1, 3). The act of speaking was God's act of authority. It brings things into being things that were not. Speaking's first principle is to bring light (Gen. 1:3). While research tells us people retain the least amount of information through verbal communication (Lou, 2012, p. S38), yet it is God's preferred method of propagating truth because the vessel is called to be a manifestation of the very truth he preaches. Preaching thus carries with it a nonverbal power that cannot be replicated in any other way (1 Cor. 2:4). Jesus' teaching was supercharged because "the Word became flesh" (John 1:1; Mark 1:22). The religious leaders couldn't touch Jesus' authority because the Word was not embodied in them. Yet when Jesus spoke, the Word came with force because it had already been realized in His life. This incarnational principle is at the heart of why God chose speaking to be His main tool of church planting. Preaching is meant to convey the truth that has been humanized and actualized in the preacher.

This also explains Jesus' ferocity against the Pharisees and Sadducees' collective hypocrisy (Matt. 23:13-33). Their proclivity to preach the truth without demonstrating it was the opposite of the incarnational principle. Their way of living gutted this principle and served to dishearten the people. They could not preach life because they didn't have life in them. They were vipers sucking the life out of people (Matt. 13:33).

The early apostles also understood that the core of their ministry and the key to the founding of the first church rested on preaching. Acts 2:42 put preaching as the first priority in community building. When the issue of serving widows came up in the fast-growing church, they decided against it in order to stay focused on "prayer and the ministry of the word" (Acts 6:4). Their conclusion was, "It is not desirable for us to neglect the word of God in order to serve tables" (Acts 6:2). It may have been reasonable and laudable if the apostles had chosen to serve the widows, but they understood the appointed task of preaching was even more important. That was a pivotal and wise decision.

Jesus told the disciples that John the Baptist was the Elijah to come (Matt. 11:14), yet John did not have the ministry of miracles that Elijah had. There is not a single record of a miracle which John performed (John 10:41). In what sense then was John, Elijah? It was in his authority. John's authority was his preaching. It was his preaching that galvanized the nation and triggered an avalanche of repentance. What was John doing all those years in the desert? He was studying and consecrating himself to God's Word. He fasted and prayed so the Word would come alive in his heart and mind with the sharpness of a two-edged sword. He had to feel what God felt. He had to think about what God thought. John would receive the revolutionary message of the kingdom so he could trumpet it from the banks of the Jordan River.

In choosing John, God prioritized preaching over miracles. Of course, this is not to diminish the ministry of miracles in any way. Jesus was the greatest miracle worker ever. God just chose a narrower skill set for John. Preaching would be primary. We see then why Jesus focused so deeply on studying the Scriptures and understanding truth at a very early age. Preaching is the quintessential skill of a planter. It's preaching that breaks the yoke. It's preaching that breaks the strongholds in people's minds. It's preaching that sets people free. It's preaching that disrupts. When Jesus quoted Isaiah 61:1-2 in His sermon at Nazareth (Luke 4:18), Isaiah foretold that the anointing would work through declaration and proclamation. Words spoken from God are liberating. When does a church become a church? When there is a set preacher.

With this Paul agreed. His writing is replete with the primacy of preaching. To Timothy, he said, "Preach the word, be ready in season and out of season; reprove, rebuke, exhort, with great patience and instruction" (2 Tim. 4:2). This was a reinforcement of his earlier exhortation to Timothy to "teach and preach" (1 Tim. 6:2). Paul said of himself that he was "appointed a preacher and an apostle and a teacher," showing Paul's own self-awareness that his ministry as a church planter was tied to preaching (2 Tim. 1:11; 1 Tim. 2:7). To Titus, Paul said, "Exhort and reprove with all authority" (Titus 2:15). And when it came to installing new elders in the church, the one skill in Paul's list, among the required character traits, was the ability to teach (1 Tim. 3:2; Titus 1:9). The government of God rests on preaching because it's the originating point from which the kingdom flows forth.

PAUL: EQUIPPED AND QUALIFIED

"I [was] educated under Gamaliel" (Acts 22:3).

As seen in the preceding discussion, Paul understood the high call of preaching. Like Jesus, Paul gave himself to education and deep learning. From the ages of fourteen to twenty, Paul studied under Gamaliel, the leading Pharisee of his time (Bruce, 1977, p. 43). The normal learning process in rabbinical schools of that time was to engage in regular and rigorous debate (Cohen, 1949, p. x). This was a time-tested method for honing one's mind and testing one's mastery of the Torah in the arena of argumentation. It served to develop a student's ability to think quickly on his feet, and the ability to "preach in the moment." Out of this training method, Paul emerged as a champion debater, and one who was "advancing in Judaism beyond many of my contemporaries among my countrymen" (Gal. 1:14). Paul's foundation for becoming an outstanding preacher was set.

DUAL CITIZENSHIP

In addition to his grasp of Scriptures, Paul was also broadly equipped to be an international church planter. Two biographical details provide a window into Paul's qualifications. While addressing the mob that protested his presence in the temple at Jerusalem, Paul stated, "I am a Jew from Tarsus, in Cilicia, a citizen of no mean city" (Acts 21:36-39). Then, a bit later, he added he was also a Roman citizen (Acts 22:27-28). That Paul was a citizen of both Tarsus and the Roman Empire provides valuable detail about his upbringing and background.

Tarsus was a city of prominence as it was the appointed capital of Cilicia, a province that was part of Rome's jurisdiction. It was situated approximately two hundred miles northwest of Jerusalem. As part of the

Roman Empire, Tarsus enjoyed many privileges including exemption from imperial taxes (Bruce, 1977, p. 34). Because Tarsus was a Greek-speaking city, Paul grew up at least bilingual, speaking both Aramaic (his mother tongue, being from a devout Jewish home) and Greek (Bruce, 1977, pp. 42–43). As a scholar of the Torah, Paul would have also been well versed in Hebrew. And it's not without possibility that Paul was acquainted with Latin, the other official language of the Roman Empire. In total, Paul could have been adept in four languages.

Besides being a city of political standing, Tarsus was also culturally and educationally influential. It was said that "the people were avid in the pursuit of culture" and gave themselves "to the study of philosophy, the liberal arts and the whole round of learning in general ... [even surpassing] Athens and Alexandria" as a university city of repute (Bruce, 1977, p. 35). Additionally, Tarsus was a city of wealth. By virtue of its proximity to fertile lands, it was known for its flax and goat hair that gave rise to its popular linens and water-resistant outerwear. As a city of means, some of the citizens were described as "addicted to luxury, levity and insolence," all common features of worldly city life (Bruce, 1977, p. 35).

From his Tarsian roots, we can see that Paul was immersed in the buzz and activity of metropolitan culture. He would have innately understood the dark side of cities as well as their potential. He understood a city's power to influence and spread culture to surrounding regions.

Being a citizen of Tarsus also indicated that Paul's family was in some measure well-to-do, as citizenship only came by ownership of property. Thus, while Paul comported himself in the humblest of means throughout his ministry, he was acquainted with wealth and the privilege of wealth. This was another equipping that would give him the facility in reaching the entire spectrum of society—from the poorest to the wealthiest.

Paul was also a Roman citizen. Those who possessed this citizenship were afforded the highest level of rights in the empire, including the right to fair public trials, exclusion from certain punishments given to commoners, and protection from blanket execution orders (Bruce, 1977, p. 39). As F. F. Bruce writes, "Among the citizens and other residents of Tarsus, the few Roman citizens, whether Greeks or Jews by birth, would [have] constitute[d] [the] social elite" (Bruce, 1977, p. 38). Paul would utilize his Roman status with great purpose—socially, legally, and for the kingdom—as he used this citizenship to travel freely as a church planter throughout Rome's vast territories.

PAUL THE TENTMAKER

Vocationally, Paul was a maker of tents (Acts 18:3). Coming from Cilicia, he would have worked with cilicium, which was a kind of luxury fabric used for tents and saddles (Long, 2015). Acquiring a marketplace skill was a common practice for rabbis. They did this so they could teach the people without charging any fees (Bruce, 1977, p. 220). Tentmaking was a profitable skill to have as Aquila and Priscilla, two of Paul's beloved coworkers, owned a tentmaking business with outlets in Rome, Corinth, and Ephesus (Bruce, 1977, pp. 250–251). Because of this, Paul would have been versed in the marketplace and the particulars of running a business. But more importantly, being able to make tents offered Paul a way to support himself and not have the worry of depending on outside sources for help.

From all this, we have a broad view of Paul's qualifications. He was cross-culturally adept, socioeconomically at ease, linguistically gifted, business-aware, and versed in the complexities of cosmopolitan life. From politics to morality to education to public discourse, Paul was the complete leadership package. And in that, we find how the work of church planting is not to be taken lightly, but instead is to be approached with preparation and dedication so the planter has the requisite skills to be successful.

ACTIVATION—CAPABILITY (#3)

1. List jobs and experiences that have given you skills and experiences that you believe will help you in planting.
2. Of the skills you possess, list your top five skills as a planter.
3. As best as you can, list the reason why people follow you. Ask people for their opinion, if necessary.
4. What are you doing to grow yourself? Have you experienced plateaus? How did you break through?

7

Key #4 — Consecration: The Key to Your Plant

"I am in the Father, and the Father is in me" (John 14:10).

There can be no plant without a consecrated leader. God wants to do a deep work in the planter so the planter can plant a deep work in God.

A MAN OF RIGHTEOUSNESS AND OBEDIENCE

Jesus' story of consecration began even before he was born. As announced to Mary (Jesus' mother), the angel Gabriel stated in no uncertain terms that the boy would be great and called the Son of the Most High. David's throne would be given to Him, and His kingdom would have no end (Luke 1:32-33). Soon after His birth, eight days in when his parents brought Him to the temple to be dedicated, more prophesies followed as Simeon and Anna spoke of the redemptive ministry that would mark His life (Luke 2:22-38). Later, as Jesus grew to the age of accountability, Isaiah prophesied of how the Christ child would learn to "refuse evil and choose good" (Isa. 7:14-16). Jesus would walk in righteousness from his earliest days to his last. His life would be one of continuous holiness and devotion.

Jesus knew how to abide in the Father, and He in turn taught the disciples to abide in Him (John 15:4). "I am the vine, you are the branches; he who abides in Me and I in him, he bears much fruit, for apart from Me you can do nothing" (John 15:5). Jesus' own consecration to the Father would be the inspiration for the disciples' consecration to Him.

Jesus never did anything unless He saw the Father doing it (John 5:19). He never said anything unless He heard the Father saying it (John 8:28). He did nothing on His own initiative (John 8:28). He was a man in step with God (John 6:38). He was obedient to the Father in all things, even unto His death on the cross (Phil. 2:8). He was wholly committed to God's glory (John 17:4; 8:50).

A MAN OF THE SPIRIT

Jesus was also a man given to the Holy Spirit and His promptings. He took time to talk with Nicodemus because, despite the lateness of the night, Jesus sensed the "wind was blowing" in the religious leader's life (John 3:8). He conversed with the woman at the well even though He was weary and hungry because there would be "food in doing the Father's will" (John 4:31-34). The first peek of His glory would be at an un-planned wedding moment when He felt God working through His mother's insistence to turn the water into wine (John 2:4, 11). These situations were but an ongoing sample of a life that was continuously led and governed by the Spirit.

A MAN WITHOUT SIN

Jesus was tempted by the devil like none other. The devil offered Jesus all the kingdoms of the world. Jesus said no (Matt. 4:8-10). The devil tempted Jesus to succumb to pride by using His miracle-working powers to turn stones into bread. Jesus said no (Matt. 4:2-4). God even allowed the devil to transport Jesus to the pinnacle of the temple, where the devil challenged Jesus to test God's love for Him. Jesus said no (Matt. 4:5-7). Jesus was tempted in every way, yet without sin (Heb. 4:15). Jesus could say as no one has ever been able to say, "The ruler of this world … has nothing in Me" (John 14:30).

Jesus was untainted morally. His character and integrity were perfect. There were no grounds by which people or the devil could diminish His spiritual authority or stature. No devices conceived against Him would prevail. He had no issues with women, with money, with fame, with power—issues that all too often sabotage a leader. In fact, in all these areas He provided the opposite example. He set the standard in how to treat women, how to steward finances, and how to exercise power. Rather than being a liability or behaving in a way that called the church's reputation into question, He raised people's hope and admiration for what the church could be. His character was the foundation of the church. As King David stated, "Righteousness and justice are the foundation of your throne" (Ps. 89:14). Later, David's son Solomon would echo this same sentiment: "His throne will be established in righteousness" (Prov. 25:5).

Jesus was consecrated in every way, which made Him the perfect church planter. God chose Him to be the head of the church and its chief cornerstone (Eph. 1:20, 22). Consecration is a work of the Spirit in concert with the Word. God's purpose is to shape the planter's life and lifestyle so it will reflect the glory of God and the gospel. It's the essential foundation of every planter's ministry.

PAUL: INNER LIFE

"For you have died and your life is hidden with Christ in God" (Col. 3:3).

Paul's "rate of planting" and the speed with which he established churches was astounding. While estimates vary as to how many churches he planted (Cole, n.d.; Porta, 2013); conservatively, we can say he personally planted nine churches in a ten-year period. On his first missionary tour, churches were planted in Pisidian Antioch, Iconium, Lystra, and Derbe. On his second trip, he planted in Philippi, Thessalonica, Berea, and Corinth. On his third trip, the church in Ephesus was established. That's a total of nine. If averaged over the ten-year window, this means Paul planted a new church every thirteen months. However, the actual rate of planting on the first and second trips was closer to four months (Porta, 2013). (He spent one to two years each in Corinth and Ephesus, thus "skewing" the average.)

LIVING LETTER

How could Paul achieve such a rapid rate? More will be said about this later, but one of the key reasons relates to the issue of consecration. Just as

Paul complimented the Corinthians as being a "living letter" (2 Cor. 3:3), so Paul himself was a "living letter" penned by the Holy Spirit to each new congregation he planted. They had a vivid picture in their minds of what a Christian should look like, how he should act, what motivated him, and his love for God. While new congregants would have been "young babes" in Christ, nevertheless, they had a constant visual of one who was always "[pressing] on toward the goal for the prize of the upward call of God in Christ Jesus," and one who "counted all things as loss in view of the surpassing value of knowing Christ Jesus my Lord" (Phil. 3:8, 12). If a picture is worth a thousand words, then in Paul's case, it was worth a thousand sermons.

While taking four months to a year to establish a church seems mind-bending, yet in light of the "picture" left behind, we can see why a budding church could continue on and thrive after such a short start-up period. Paul said on numerous occasions, "Be imitators of me, just as I also am of Christ" (1 Cor. 11:1; 4:16; 2 Thes. 3:7, 9; 1 Tim. 4:12; Titus 2:7; 1 Thes. 1:6). His own life was an ongoing "virtual teaching tool" for believers. This was also Jesus' strategy in calling the twelve disciples to be with Him in His travels. It was so they would forever have a picture in their minds of a man of God and how he lived.

CANVAS TIME

God takes time in preparing His servants. Just as an artist takes time to paint a masterpiece, so God puts great effort into the "canvases" He's going to put on display. A masterpiece will keep the crowds coming back again and again—to look at, to gaze upon, to ponder, to enjoy, and to be inspired; but a sloppy portrait will attract no attention.

We see God's strategy in keeping Jesus hidden for thirty years, as well as the purpose behind Paul's twelve years of behind-the-scenes preparation prior to his planting efforts. God had to get the picture right. The goal was to make the messenger and the message indistinguishable. Paul's life would be indistinguishable from the gospel and the gospel would be indistinguishable from Paul.

This is why Paul was keen to share with the Colossians this major truth of the cross: "For you have died and your life is hidden in Christ"

(Col. 3:3). The goal was not for people to see how great of a planter Paul was. The goal was for people to see how great Christ was in the planter. We are hidden but Christ is revealed. For this to happen, much brokenness must take place. Personal ambitions, weaknesses, sins, self-centeredness, vanity, insecurity, and pride must be dealt with. To be a disruptor, one must experience God's disruption. That disruption is part of the consecration process. The dross must be brought to the surface so impurities can be removed. Cleansing results in the earthen vessel being sanctified for the Master's use (2 Tim. 2:20-21).

If your life is built on the rock, then you can plant a church that is founded on the rock. No rain, flood, or wind will cause it to fall down (Matt. 7:24-25). Your consecration is the key to establishing a strong and enduring work.

ACTIVATION—CONSECRATION (#4)

1. Describe a significant season in your life when God broke you.
2. Describe the most difficult step of obedience you've taken.
3. Share an example of how your walk has inspired someone else.

Phase II

Construction (New Plant)

8

Key #5—Core Team: Finding Those Who Will Plant with Me

"He called His disciples to Himself and chose twelve of them" (Luke 6:13).

The Bible speaks often of Jesus praying (Mark 1:35; Matt. 14:23; Luke 5:16). But in only one place does it speak of Jesus spending all night in prayer. That was when He chose who would be on his core team. Luke 6:12–13 records, "It was at this time that He went off to the mountain to pray, and He spent the whole night in prayer to God. And when day came, He called His disciples to Him and chose twelve of them, whom He also named as apostles." Who will be on a planting team is of paramount importance. They help set the bar. They help lay the foundations. They help establish the culture. They provide comfort and encouragement. They provide wisdom and insight. They help shape the mission. The composition of the planting team is absolutely essential.

Of the hundreds and thousands of people that followed Jesus, many would have been quality candidates. Who would Jesus choose? Bright ones? Wealthy ones? Charismatic ones? Connected ones? What would be the criteria? And how many should be chosen? The options were many.

Jesus' popularity was surging. He was going "viral." Suggestions must have abounded in Jesus' ear as to possible candidates, not to mention those volunteering themselves be on His team. But this was clearly not to be an exercise in human wisdom. The decision required the Holy Spirit's wisdom. This would require seeking God all night. He had to get it right.

Just as God had told Samuel not to look on the outward but on the heart (1 Sam. 16:7), so God would have to reveal to Jesus who had the right ingredients. Jesus could not judge as Samuel did on the basis of physical characteristics, what seemed appealing to the eye, or what the people wanted. This selection was too important to be left to chance.

In the end, the Father spoke definitively to Jesus (Luke 6:13-16;

John 13:18), and those Jesus chose provides an important commentary on the criteria we should use in recruiting our own core team.

First, Jesus chose those who would be "all in" (Luke 14:25-33; 9:61-62). They would be ones who had counted the cost and were willing to leave everything to go after Him (Matt. 4:19-21; Luke 18:28). They would heed the invitation to take up their cross, deny themselves, and follow Him (Luke 9:23). These would be the "worthy" ones (Matt. 10:38). These would give their lives for the mission.

Second, Jesus had to choose men with great loyalty. This is closely related to the first criteria yet is distinct. One can be all in for a mission (point #1), but not be loyal to the person leading the mission. In battle, a soldier may subscribe to the rationale for war but might never follow his commander if given a personal choice. However, if one is loyal to a leader, no matter the mission of the leader, he will be faithful because of his love for the one he follows. For eleven out of the twelve disciples, this was true. They were fiercely loyal, even pledging to die with Jesus (Mark 14:31). Although they would stumble in this (Mark 14:27, 50) Jesus understood their hearts, and as history records, they would later all die as martyrs (save John).

The lone failure was Judas. Jesus' handling of money greatly incensed Judas because Judas loved money and didn't approve of Jesus' "wasteful" acceptance of expensive perfume that was poured out over His feet (John 12:1-8). In Judas's mind, Jesus had gone too far. The perfume should have been sold to help the poor instead of allowing an act of lavishness to take place. He felt justified to commit his act of betrayal (Mark 14:10-11). But in reality, Judas was only wanting to line his pockets with the money that would have gone into the ministry account because he was a pilferer (John 12:6). He was just deceiving himself. So with a kiss, Judas gave Jesus up to the authorities (Luke 22:48). Yet despite Judas' disloyalty and the great heartache this brought to Jesus, the sovereignty of God still used Judas' sin to fulfill His redemptive purposes.

Third, Jesus chose His men on the basis of team chemistry. Of the twelve disciples Jesus selected, half of them were men who came from the same hometown or region, and four out of the twelve were two sets of brothers (Luke 6:14; John 1:44; Matt. 4:18-20). Additionally, seven out of the twelve were of the same profession, being fisherman (John 21:1-3). This speaks of the premium Jesus put on team dynamics, ease of relationship, comfort level, the similarity of background, and how all this would fuel a strong unity and camaraderie. They had a big job ahead, and Jesus chose men in such a way as to optimize their ability to love one another, respect one another, and show mutual submission one to another.

Fourth, Jesus chose those who were teachable. These would be men who would undergo intense training in order to lead the church. And they would need to be men who could see the Old Testament with New Testament eyes and not be bound to old truth that Jesus would soon replace at the Cross.

Fifth, Jesus chose men with whom He liked to hang out. They would be His friends, not His employees (John 15:15). They would do life together—eat, drink, sleep, walk, talk, and have fun together. They would celebrate together and retreat together (Mark 6:31-32). They would ex-perience high and lows and have common "war stories" to tell. "Do you remember when Jesus was asleep in the boat, and we all thought we were going to sink?" (see Mark 4:38-40). "Do you remember when we thought leaven referred to actual bread that the Pharisees and Sadducees made? We were so clueless!" (Matt. 16:5-7). "And remember when Jesus told us to feed the five thousand? Did you see the look on Philip's face? He went white on us!" (John 6:6-7). Such were the good times. Jesus was glad to make memories with them.

Sixth, Jesus chose those who were spiritually hungry. As forthcoming leaders of the new church, they had to be spiritually passionate men. Their followers needed to see and know their leaders were on fire for Jesus, especially in light of the persecution they would face. An apathetic spirit would have been an automatic disqualification from being chosen. Jesus had to choose men who were curious, eager to grow, and desirous of emulating His life. When Jesus prayed, the disciples said, "Lord, teach us to pray" (Luke 11:1). This must have warmed Jesus' heart, knowing they were wanting to go deeper. Biblically speaking, despite the disciples' reputation for being unlearned and uneducated, they were far from being theologically illiterate. On the contrary, they were adroit, informed, and had much of the Old Testament on recall. Peter preached spontaneously from Joel at Pentecost, and the decision regarding circumcision was mediated by a collective understanding of the "tabernacle of David," which was a fresh application from Amos 9:11-12 (Acts 15:16). Additionally, we see the disciples were devoted to constant study of the Word, so as to be able to feed the exploding church in Jerusalem

(Acts 6:4). We thus see how spiritual hunger was an important metric Jesus used to choose his core team.

Seventh, Jesus had to choose men of good character and sound integrity. The gospel could not be soiled or brought into disrepute by misbehavior or moral failure. Jesus envisioned a church without spot or wrinkle, and this had to start with the leaders. All twelve turned out just as Jesus anticipated, with no stumbles in regard to money, sex, fame, drink, addictions, marriage, parenting, and more. They stuck together, ministered together, were accountable to each other, and lived and died together. Their reputations and names were regarded with "high esteem" (Acts 5:13). They had moral authority because their lives were pure and holy.

Eighth, Jesus chose men who could preach well. Again, we see in Acts 6:4 how the apostles saw their primary role as preachers and teachers. While Peter and John are most prominently showcased in Scripture for their oratory and speaking, we can deduce from this verse that all the disciples were anointed to communicate the Word of the Lord with life and power. As they preached in the temple and circulated from house to house, all were absorbed with the job of feeding the flock (Acts 2:46; 5:42). They were all needed to cover the multitude of home meetings happening in Jerusalem while the church was growing exponentially (Acts 2:41, 43; 4:4). Jesus had to choose great communicators, and clearly the disciples did their job well as "the word of God kept on spreading; and the number of the disciples continued to increase greatly in Jerusalem, and a great many of the priests were becoming obedient to the faith" (Acts 6:7). Because Jesus chose well, the church prospered well.

There are few joys greater than having a team with which to change the world. A band of brothers and sisters is priceless. The march toward impact must be built with those who will care deeply with you about the mission.

PAUL: ASSEMBLING TALENT

"He took Timothy" (Acts 16:3).

Just as Barnabas recruited Paul to be part of the Antioch leadership team (Acts 11:25-26), so Paul would turn around and do likewise in recruiting people to his team during his three church planting tours. With the Antioch experience in hand, Paul understood the intrinsic value of creating teams, the camaraderie in it, and the strength that came from working together. Through his approximately ten years of active ministry (AD 48–57), Paul was keen to have those of kindred spirit join him in advancing the kingdom. Of the many young apostles that Paul trained, three, in particular, are profiled here.

SILAS

After the unfortunate separation of Barnabas and Paul, Silas was selected by Paul to accompany him on his second tour (Acts 15:40). Knowing the rigors required of traveling and planting new churches, Paul would have been very deliberate in choosing who should be part of his team. Silas was already a proven and trusted worker, having been tasked along with Judas to assist in communicating the Jerusalem Council's decision (Acts 15:22). Silas's profile was very similar to Barnabas's in that Silas also carried the heart and good standing of the Jerusalem apostles. Silas created a linkage and continuity between what was happening in Jerusalem and what was to further unfold through Paul. That Silas had the same spiritual DNA as Barnabas was also crucial for Paul, as he wanted to carry on the same spirit and foundations that he and Barnabas had brought to the churches during their first tour. For Silas to be chosen by the apostles to go to Antioch—as they did with Barnabas (Acts 11:22)—spoke highly of Silas's ability to work cross-culturally among the Gentiles, another important qualification for Paul as this was his primary field. Like Barnabas, Silas was a recognized prophet (Acts 15:32), which Paul would later state was critical in planting churches (Eph. 2:20). Silas may have been recruited by Paul for his established credentials, but Silas also distinguished himself in other important ways.

In responding to the Macedonian call (Acts 16:9-10), Paul and Silas quickly found good soil in Philippi as God opened Lydia's heart by the riverside (Acts 16:13-14). Spiritual warfare, however, followed quickly as Paul confronted a spirit of divination and the two servants of God were beaten and thrown in jail, complete with feet shackled in chains (Acts 16:22-24). But instead of commiserating in their circumstances, the two sang hymns of praise heartily unto the Lord (Acts 16:25). In response to their choruses, a powerful earthquake occurred, and after a few chaotic hours, the jailer in charge of the prisoners and his entire household got saved. This crazy sequence of events revealed the quality of man that Silas proved to be. Right along with Paul, he took his blows for Christ. Right along with Paul, he praised God with gusto. This was a man that Paul could lean on no matter the circumstances.

When Paul and Silas went on to Thessalonica, they again faced strong opposition, but Silas proved fearless, just like he did in Philippi (Acts 17:5). In Berea, the team saw many come to the Lord as Silas's evangelistic spirit was a great complement to Paul's (Acts 17:10-12). Later when Silas was separated from Paul, he continued to support Paul until they were reunited in Corinth (Acts 18:5). His loyalty was a comfort to Paul and allowed Paul to exercise his gifts with great effectiveness (Acts 18:5). Paul's choice of Silas was an excellent one, and Silas's many qualities proved a perfect match for the tasks they faced together.

TIMOTHY

Shortly after Paul had selected Silas, he chose Timothy (Acts 16:1-3), and as Acts would record, this core group of three would go on to provide some of the best highlights in Paul's ministry as they planted churches in Philippi, Thessalonica, Berea, and Corinth on the second tour. Their unity, brotherhood, and love were evident throughout their time together and Timothy would later become a key legacy of Paul's ministry.

Although Timothy was still a young missionary, Paul sensed in him a call to apostolic ministry. Timothy came from a godly heritage and was taught the ways of the Torah from childhood (2 Tim. 1:5; 3:14-15). He had an excellent spirit (1 Tim. 4:12; Acts 16:1-3). Having a Jewish mother and Gentile father, Timothy represented the new covenant message "in the flesh." As he worked alongside Paul, a father-son relationship emerged strongly (2 Tim. 1:2; 1 Tim. 1:2; Phil. 2:22) and Timothy became deeply loyal to Paul through thick and thin (Acts 17:14-15; 18:5). Paul implicitly trusted Timothy and was sent by Paul to many of the churches for follow-up ministry (1 Cor. 4:17; Phil. 2:23; 1 Thess. 3:2). Later, Timothy would pastor the church in Ephesus, one of Paul's most significant works (1 Tim. 1:3).

As a young leader, Timothy was given to timidity (2 Tim. 1:7) and didn't have the same aggressive evangelistic spirit as Paul (2 Tim. 4:5). But Paul encouraged him to be strong in his calling in light of the prophetic words spoken over his life (1 Tim. 1:18). Timothy was a wonderful teacher and preacher (2 Cor. 1:19; 1 Tim. 4:16; 2 Tim. 2:15; 4:2), spiritually gifted (1 Tim. 4:14), deeply pastoral (Phil. 2:20), servant-hearted (Acts 19:22), and possessed an exemplary character (1 Tim. 4:12; 6; 11). He was observant, teachable, and had fully assimilated Paul's example (2 Tim. 3:10). In keeping with his mentor, Timothy knew how to suffer persecution and experienced his own imprisonment (2 Tim. 2:3-5; 3:12; Heb. 13:23). He became a proven and inspiring leader in his own right (Phil. 2:23). In the end, Paul paid Timothy the highest of compliments by stating of him that, "I have no one else of kindred spirit" (Phil. 2:20). Indeed, Timothy would be listed as a coauthor in six of Paul's thirteen letters (Phil. 1:1; Col. 1:1; 2 Cor. 1:1; 1 Thess. 1:1; 2 Thess. 1:1; Philem. 1:1). Paul's selection of Timothy to be on his team was one of his best ministry decisions ever.

TITUS

Like Silas and Timothy, Titus featured prominently in Paul's life. And like Timothy, Titus was a "true child in the faith" (Titus 1:4). Titus possessed a Greek lineage similar to Timothy's (Gal. 2:3). Thus, two of Paul's most important disciples were living examples of the message of grace that Paul so passionately preached. Titus was recruited by Paul shortly after his first planting tour, and Paul took him along with Barnabas to the Jerusalem Council (Gal. 2:1). The exact details of Paul's first meetings with Titus are not recorded, but his relationship and love for Titus were evident in his second letter to the Corinthians, when he shared he had had "no rest for my spirit, not finding Titus" in Troas (2 Cor. 2:12-13), and the subsequent comfort he had received after being reunited with him (2 Cor. 7:6). Titus was an integral part of Paul's team and acted as a troubleshooter on behalf of Paul when Paul was going through intense relational strains with the Corinthian church (2 Cor. 7:7-15). Titus also served as ambassador in the delicate matter of receiving offerings from the church for the impoverished brother and sisters in Jerusalem (2 Cor. 8:1-7; Rom. 15:25-26).

As part of Paul's team, Titus was given pastoral oversight for the churches in Crete, being reminded by Paul to establish proper church government by setting in elders there. Titus had authority to "reprove severely... rebellious men, empty talkers and deceivers, especially those of the circumcision," as they were "upsetting whole families" in the churches (Titus 1:10-13). Paul trusted Titus to execute disciplinary actions and to establish a sense of order through sound preaching and proper modeling (Titus 2:1, 7-8).

In Titus, we see another example of how Paul enlarged his ministry through quality disciples and created an impact beyond what he could have done by himself. Having an excellent core team was essential to Paul in his planting efforts.

ACTIVATION—CORE TEAM (#5)

1. Recount an experience when you've been on a great team. Name three things you really liked about it. What other things do you want to develop on your team?
2. Who is on your core team right now?
3. Does each of them care as deeply as you want them to? If not, will you let them go or try to improve them? If you want to improve them, what is your plan?
4. Finding great talent is one of the most difficult tasks in building a world-class organization. What keys would you pass on to others to attract the best?

9

Key #6—Culture: How Will This Plant Work, Look, and Feel?

"I will build my church" (Matt. 16:18).

THE POWER OF SMALL

As stated in Chapter 3, God loves to use the unsuspecting, lowly, and despised things of this world to make a statement (1 Cor. 1:26-29). He loves to use the humble, insignificant, and small to do great things. Sarah was barren. Moses was a murderer. Rahab was a harlot. Ruth was a Moabite. Jeremiah was a teenager. Elisha was bald-headed. Amos was a sycamore fig grower. Josiah was a boy. David was overlooked. Peter and John were uneducated. Jesus was born in a manger.

In keeping with this theme, Jesus gave us the parables of the mustard seed and of the leaven to describe the kingdom (Matt. 13:31-33). In the mustard seed picture, Jesus pointed out how the kingdom is "smaller than all other seeds; but when it is full-grown, it is larger than the garden plants and becomes a tree" (Matt. 13:32). In the yeast picture, Jesus stated that the kingdom was "hid (unseen) in three pecks of meal until it was all leavened" (Matt. 13:33). With these two pictures, Jesus shows us there are two kinds of churches in the kingdom: (1) small grows big (mustard seed); or (2) small *is* big (leaven). Size is not the issue. Impact is the goal. Small or big can create impact. Small or big can be influential. Small or big can make a difference. The secret is having the right DNA. This is where the culture of an organization is set.

NEW TESTAMENT LEADERSHIP

Another way to express how kingdom DNA is established is to see it from the Ephesians 4:11-13 paradigm. In this passage, the Bible states that Jesus divided his leadership mantle, or his governmental responsibilities (Isa. 9:6), into five offices: apostle, prophet, evangelist, pastor, and teacher. From these five spheres of leadership, we can see how church culture is shaped and established. First, the church must be missional (apostolic). It must be about the business of the Great Commission (Matt. 28:19-20). It must dream big. It must be enterprising and risk-taking. It must be looking to new frontiers and advancing the kingdom. It must be visionary. Second, the church must be passionately Christ-centered, dwelling richly in the Word, and nurturing a deep Spirit-enriched life. She represents God's voice and heart in the earth (prophetic). Third, the church must have a passion for souls, seeking to win the lost wherever they may be (evangelistic). The church is called to be fishers of men. Fourth, the church must be a caring, kind, and loving community, a place where new believers can grow and flourish in becoming disciples (pastoral). It is a place of freedom and safety. Fifth, the church must excel in the knowledge of God (2 Peter 3:18). Learning and being diligent students of Scripture are key to spiritual maturity and growth (teaching). In aggregate, these five offices shape the goals, values, planning, rhythms, activities, budgets, operations, behavior (appearance, dress, habits), speech, and public persona of the church.

EMPOWERING THE WHOLE CHURCH

But the model doesn't stop there. While the leadership culture is crucial, there is a larger organizational aim to be achieved, as this model is designed to empower the *entire* body of Christ. Just as Jesus mobilized, trained, and empowered his Twelve to do the work of the ministry (Matt. 10; Luke 10), so Ephesians 4 leaders are tasked with creating a wave of ministry and impact *through* an empowered people. The leaders are pebbles dropped into the water, but the people are the ripples radiating out.

This is called a servant-leadership culture, in which everyone is mobilized to do the work of the ministry (Mark 10:45). This is not the

Pareto principle where 20 percent of the people do 80 percent of the work. This is the kingdom principle of 100 percent of the people doing 100 percent of the work. Servant-leaders recognize, celebrate, and release people with their diversity of gifts, talents, and callings inside *and* outside the church to bring glory to God. First Corinthians 12 refers to this as the whole body joyfully contributing to the whole mission. Each person is valued and treasured. No one is left behind in kingdom culture.

THE CHURCH GROWS UP

Then there is a third aspect given in this passage: not only is there to be a strong leadership and a vibrant ministry culture, the church is also to have a culture of maturity and stature which mirrors the "fullness of Christ" (Eph. 4:13). When nonbelievers come to the church, there must be a different sense, a different vibe in the air. This is not the world as they know it. It represents another place. It's joyful, peaceful, engaging, delightful, authentic, love-filled, free, clean, powerful, and compelling—which is to say, it feels like Jesus is here because Christ is formed in the members (Gal. 4:19). This is a body that has "grown up into all aspects into Him, who is the head, even Christ" (Eph. 4:16).

With these three priorities, Jesus defines for us the type of culture He is looking to establish—great leadership, great service, great maturity.

PAUL: INSPIRED ARCHITECT

"Like a wise master builder, I laid a foundation" (1 Cor. 3:10).

Paul the Planter

Given the kingdom DNA that Jesus established, how did Paul go about establishing churches? What does a Pauline church look like? Critical to this answer is Paul's recognition of the gracing that was in him: "I planted, Apollos watered, but God was causing the growth" (1 Cor. 3:6). In stating this, Paul recognized there were two stages in church planting:

the founding stage (Paul) and the scaling stage (Apollos). Paul's sphere of expertise was in the start-up phase. This is where he excelled. That is not to say Paul didn't know how to scale (water) or Apollos didn't know how to establish (plant), but each had their primary anointing's that acted as a complement to one another. To be sure, as Paul stated, one kind of apostle was not better than another, "Neither the one who plants nor the one who waters is anything, but God who causes the growth" (1 Cor. 3:7-8). For Paul, as a pioneering apostle, this framed what a Pauline church looked like and the fruit left by Paul's ministry bears this out. It also created the trajectory for how Pauline churches would work, look, and feel.

CHARACTERISTICS OF A PAULINE CHURCH

First, Pauline churches don't have long planting timelines. As noted previously, Paul had the ability to establish churches quickly, and it was put forth that this ability was due in large part to the incarnational life he possessed. Paul's life was so Spirit infused that his personal presence and ministry were like pouring out fresh oxygen everywhere he went. The breeze he brought was the breeze of heaven. The anointing on his life was not just something to behold, it had impartational power (Rom. 1:11). Whereas it may take a thousand sermons from a scribe to understand a particular truth, with Paul one immediately caught what he was saying because of the presence he carried. Paul's physical person had such transformational power that handkerchiefs which touched his body could be carried away, placed on the sick and they would be healed (Acts 19:11). This was exactly the same power that Jesus carried when the woman with the issue of blood touched the fringe of Jesus' garment and was made well (Matt. 9:20). These two men's lives radiated with so much life, even the material clothes they wore caught their power. Thus, with a vessel like Paul roaming the land, it was no wonder planting churches was a "quick work."

Second, Pauline churches aim to raise up local leadership. Paul's goal was to work himself out of a job right from the start. His passion was to see national leaders installed. He never saw himself in a tenured way. This is not to say planters who stay with one church their entire life are in error in any way, nor is it saying a planter who has an extended tenure is in the wrong. All are as legitimate as the other because any call of God is "right." However, Paul's template was to raise up and turn over leadership responsibilities as soon as they could be commended to the grace of God (Acts 20:32; 14:23). This was the metric Paul learned at Antioch (Acts 11:23).

Third, Paul's planting operations were "lean and mean." His teams were nimble, quick to pivot, self-financed in many cases, and could move from planting to planting with relative speed. They had humble expectations with regards to hospitality and food, and didn't carry much luggage when they traveled. Their worldly possessions were minimal. They did not expect fanfare or publicity to greet them when they came to town, and they were quick to dive into their jobs after they arrived. They were spartan in their approach and embraced a soldier's mentality (2 Tim. 2:3-4). In service of the mission, they kept things joy-filled, friendship enriched, Christ-centered, simple, practical, and uncomplicated.

Fourth, Pauline churches depend on the power of God (1 Cor. 4:20). Paul stated this in very clear terms: "My message and my preaching were not in persuasive words of wisdom, but in demonstration of the Spirit and of power, so that your faith would not rest on the wisdom of men, but on the power of God" (1 Cor. 2:4-5). The gospel was not only powerful in word but also in deed. Paul's gospel would not be anemic. Like Jesus, the gospel would be attended by signs, wonders, and miracles. These would testify that the kingdom was here and God's authority was at hand. Paul understood part of establishing an enduring faith was for new believers to see and experience God's power right from the get-go. This would establish the proper baseline of faith and view of God. This would help believers to weather the storms when they would inevitably come, knowing their God was all-powerful and able. "As you therefore have received Christ Jesus the Lord, so walk in Him" (Col. 2:6).

Fifth, Pauline churches are highly disruptive. Said those in Thessalonica, "Those who have turned the world upside down have come here" (Acts 17:6 NKJV). Wherever Paul went, disruption happened:

- Cyprus: Elymas the magician was blinded (Acts 13:11).
- Pisidian Antioch and surrounding regions: Revival breaks out, followed by intense persecution and blasphemy (Acts 13:44-45, 49-50).
- Iconium: Revival, persecution, and miracles break out (Acts 14:1-3).
- Lystra: Lame man healed, followed by the multitudes worshiping

Barnabas and Paul as Zeus and Hermes (Acts 14:10-12); Paul gets
stoned (Acts 14:19).

- Derbe: Harvest of disciples (Acts 14:21).
- Philippi: City is thrown into confusion by Paul's deliverance of
  divining girl (Acts 16:18-20).
- Thessalonica: Mobs erupt in response to Paul's teaching
  (Acts 17:5).
- Berea: Crowds attended Paul's meeting with many believing
  (Acts 17:13).
- Ephesus: Extraordinary miracles performed, followed by total chaos
  in the city (Acts 19:11, 28-34).

Power confrontations, signs and wonders, rioting, waves of revivals,
persecution, whole cities stirred—this was the effect Paul had. The
kingdom of God is disruptive. It confronts. It brings salvation. It changes
people's lives. It changes their priorities. It changes their aspirations. It
changes their motivations. It changes family structures. It changes the
marketplace. It's disruptive from top to bottom and side to side. This is
the principle of the power of the leaven; it affects the whole thing. This
is the principle of the mustard seed; the smallest of organizations (the
church plant) becomes the most significant of trees. Paul majors on
"small" because big is already programmed into it. Plant small, get big
results: this was Pauline strategy at its best.

Sixth, Pauline churches are pillars of truth (1 Tim. 3:15). False
teaching, strange doctrines, useless debates, and deceiving spirits abound,
but the church is God's reservoir of truth (1 Tim. 1:3-4; 4:1; 6:4, 20). She
is to ward off erroneous teachings so believers don't get tossed to and fro
by "every wind of doctrine" (Eph. 4:14). Disciples are made by establishing them in the knowledge that is found in Christ (Col. 3:10; Eph.
4:15, 21-24; 1 Tim. 6:3, Titus 2:1, 7, 10). Jesus made this abundantly clear
when He said in the Great Commission, "[Teach] them to obey all I have
commanded you" (Matt. 28:20).

Seventh, Pauline churches are bastions of God's grace. This, of
course, is related to the church being the pillar of truth, but this vein
deserves separate treatment. As evidenced by Paul's opening salutation
in almost every one of his letters, grace was at the forefront. There is no
gospel unless there is grace (Gal. 1:6). Grace is about extolling the
finished work of Christ. Spreading that knowledge was Paul's life's great

work. So jealous was Paul for the purity of this gospel, he invoked curses on anyone who preached a "different gospel" (Gal. 1:6-9). This message was not to be tampered with, as Jesus' work was complete and perfect, and salvation was purely by grace through faith (Eph. 2:20). No works of any kind in any manner or measure could be added to it. Religion and legalism were particularly banned from this Christ-centered gospel—even the faintest of scents (Gal. 2:11-16). The church was called to be the champion and guardian of this message. This gospel of grace would be so powerful it would conquer any stronghold that held sway over a city: hedonism (Corinth), paganism (Lystra), religion (Ephesus), asceticism (Colossae), materialism (Philippi), intellectualism (Athens), or politics (Rome). Such is the power of the cross (1 Tim. 1:11).

Eighth, Pauline churches are "locally-operated yet under authority" (Acts 14:23). Paul always operated through a father's heart (1 Cor. 4:15; 1 Thess. 2:11). As such, his relationship to the churches he planted was strongly relational, not just positional(1 Thes. 2:6-7). If authority was to be exercised, it was there when needed to protect the work or to bring course corrections (1 Thes. 5:1-11; 1 Cor. 5:1-5). Just as sons grow to be their own persons (autonomy), so Paul rejoiced to see his works thrive and mature (1 Thes. 3:6-9; Phil. 4:1). Yet as the founding father, Paul was always there to assist, encourage, and cover the work. This gave his churches the freedom to grow but the safety of knowing they had the protection and guidance of a loving father.

Ninth, Pauline churches are self-supporting. There were no funds coming from the Antioch home church to support new churches. There is nothing wrong with that kind of support; it would have been like parents helping their kids through college until they became independent. But for the new plants in Paul's time, this was not an option. This may have been due to logistical reasons. Banks back then—primitive in comparison to today's systems—did not have any technological ability to wire money or provide checking services. No websites or auto-pay links to support a cause were available. The internet was thousands of years away from being invented. So securing funds from home base would have been difficult in a practical sense. Only someone carrying cash would have made it possible. But with Paul planting churches at such a quick clip, by the time finances were brought in for a new work, Paul was already off to the next stop.

Despite this practical limitation, it seems God orchestrated this system on purpose. To be self-supporting was to stimulate ownership of the mission at the local level. There would be no wrong sense of dependence. Stipulating a self-sustaining model would teach the new members to tithe and give and become their own economic engine. This would give them their own sense of identity and pride, crucial pieces in establishing a healthy and vibrant local church. Today, with the advent of global banking and communication, we are able to raise funds ahead of time or in real-time for church-planting needs. Start-up funds are a normal routine in this day and age. There is nothing wrong with this unless there is no deadline for a church to become self-sustaining. The fundamental principle must be kept in mind: each local church should eventually become its own purse.

Tenth, Pauline churches are focused on reaching strategic city-centers and regions. This comes sharply into view during the start of Paul's second tour, when the Macedonian call came to him (Acts 16:6-10). As noted by Johnson (n.d., p. 6), the divine invitation was not to a city but to a region. God's strategy was to reach entire provinces *through* representative cities. When studying Paul's church planting footprint, it can be seen he "concentrated on the district or provincial capitals, each of which [stood] for the whole region: Philippi for Macedonia (Phil. 4:15), Thessalonica for Macedonia and Achaia (1 Thes. 1:7ff), Corinth for Achaia (1 Cor. 16:15; 2 Cor. 1:1), Ephesus for Asia (Rom. 16:5, 1 Cor. 16:19; 2 Cor. 1:8). The metropolises [were] the main centers as [far] as communication, culture, commerce, politics, and religion [were] concern[ed] (n.d., p. 7)." Planting in such cities was a way to multiply the reach of the gospel by impacting the culture that flowed out from the city to the surrounding areas. Impacting metropolises had a strong amplifying effect. Recent sociological studies show the concentration of people, infrastructure, and ideas in urban areas create a powerful exponential and catalyzing effect on innovation and wealth creation (Bettencourt, Lobo, Helbing, Kuhnert, West, 2007, p. 7301). Planting in the urban centers thus capitalizes on the momentum that comes from a critical mass of people residing in a given area.

As man of the city, Paul was uniquely equipped to reach city-centers; however, it should be stated that in the modern-day application of Paul's principles, a Pauline church can be planted anywhere (rural area or otherwise); it need not be exclusive to megacities.

Eleventh, Pauline churches love the presence of the Lord. Having grown up in the rich soil of the Antioch church, Paul would go on to reproduce the heartfelt church life he experienced there (Acts 11:19-26; 13:1-3). Worship and ministering to the Lord was foundational (first priority); hearing from the Lord was a given (prophetic); fasting was part and parcel of the corporate discipline (devotion); team leadership was multicultural and shared (unity); continuous study of the Scripture was a delight (discipleship); evangelism was a lifestyle (outflow); grace filled the air (kingdom atmosphere); and love of the brethren was all around (Christ-likeness). It was a taste of heaven on earth, with God's presence at the center of it all.

Twelfth, Pauline churches are reproducing churches. Paul not only planted churches himself, but the churches he planted also planted churches. The church in Colossae was not planted by Paul, but by Epaphras, who was part of Paul's team and was also imprisoned with him (Col. 1:7-8; Philem. 1:23). Colossae was part of a threesome of churches located in the Lycus Valley in the province of Asia, and Epaphras oversaw these churches, which included Laodicea and Hierapolis (Col. 4:12-13, 16). As a group, these churches were located approximately one hundred miles east of Ephesus, the capital of Asia—and the Ephesian church, which was founded by Paul, fed into these church plants (Bruce, 1977, p. 288). Aristarchus, one who may have been involved in the Ephesian plant (Acts 20:4) (Bruce, 1977 p. 289), was also acquainted with the Colossian saints (Col. 4:10), further speaking to the relational connection between the two churches. Paul was not only a father of churches but also a grandfather of churches.

From these points, we see Paul's master builder anointing at work (1 Cor. 3:10). His planting methods were efficient, fruitful, and impactful. His churches, like rocky-road ice cream, were to die for. That's the kind of church every planter wants to establish.

ACTIVATION—CULTURE (#6)

1. Think of churches you've been in that you loved. Why did you love them? List 3-5 reasons.
2. As planter, you get to set the culture of your church. What elements

in Jesus' or Paul's development of church culture are you most drawn to?

3. What part of a church culture do you think is most difficult to establish? And what do you think is the easiest to establish? Explain why to both questions.

10

Key #7—Creativity: Planting with Genius

"The headwaiter tasted the water which had become wine" (John 2:9).

The opening chapter of the Bible bursts with creation. From stars in the skies to ants on the ground, from soaring mountain peaks to frogs on a lily pad, from wispy clouds to fireflies around the campfire—they represent God's creativity. He is a creator from the get-go. He is not a cookie-cutter God. Not one sunset is the same. Not one snowflake is the same. Not one person is the same. God is the first original artist. It's in His blood. He is irrepressible and He loves creativity.

Jesus was no less imaginative. He did things in ways never seen before. He was a ministry artist. His ways were poetic, bold, and paradigm-breaking. He blessed those who cursed Him (Luke 6:28). He headquartered in Capernaum instead of Jerusalem (Matt. 4:13). He leveraged anonymity instead of popularity (Luke 5:14). He turned water into wine (John 2:1-11). He was born of a virgin in order to elude the reach of Adam's sin (Matt. 1:23-25). He was born in a barn with farm animals (Luke 2:7). He didn't hang out with the rich and famous but with the sinners and tax collectors (Mark 2:15-16). He chose unschooled men to be on His team (Acts 4:13). He related to women of questionable background without fear (John 4). He loved the hospitality of lepers (Matt. 26:6). He employed the quietness of a lamb (Luke 23:9). His teaching galvanized the masses as He unfolded a new covenant to them (Matt. 7:28). He cursed fig trees (Mark 11:12-14, 20-21). He was a storyteller and master communicator who spoke in parables (Mark 4:2, 11). He taught that soft is powerful (Matt. 5:3-10). He loved the multitudes and solitude at the same time (Matt. 14:21-23). He was charismatic but not eye-catching (Isa. 53:2). He loved simplicity and taught the unencumbered life (Matt. 6:19-21, 25-34). He was the master of turning natural situations into supernatural encounters

(Mark 6:33-44). He rebuked the wind and the waves and then walked on the water (Luke 8:24; John 6:19). Demons could not stand before Him (Matt. 8:28-30). He used His spit to heal people (Mark 7:33, 8:23). He wasn't bothered by continual interruptions but instead integrated them as part of his ministry (Matt. 9:20). He wasn't afraid to offend His family or the ruling powers of the day (Matt. 3:20-21, 31-34; 15:12). He mastered the "flat organization" (Luke 6:13). He started the church without a building. He financed His ministry without fundraising. His ministry had no dispersible assets when He died. He turned down invitations to be king in order to stay true to His servant call (John 6:15; Mark 10:45). He died on a cross as a "criminal." He triggered a revolution without raising a sword (Luke 22:38, 50-53). His ways were unparalleled. His creative approach took away people's breath and captured their imaginations like no one else. Jesus understood creativity. It's how He planted the church.

PAUL: NEW THINKING

"And on the Sabbath day we went outside the gate [city walls] to a riverside" (Acts 16:13).

When Paul started planting, there was no playbook to consult. No one had done it before him. There were no previous trailblazers to the Gentile world to which he could look. He would be the first to go. Paul had to rely on a mixture of common sense, ingenuity, boldness, moxie, prototyping, hard work, dedication, and Holy Spirit guidance to carry out his mission. How would he approach reaching a city? He had three general approaches.

PAUL'S THREE OVERARCHING METHODS

First, in keeping with the covenantal order established by God, Paul employed a "Jew first," or "synagogue first" approach (Rom. 1:16; Acts 13:46; 17:2). In what would be become his primary modus operandi, of the eleven target cities he visited, eight began with him going to the synagogue. During his opening tour, he went to the synagogue first in three cities:

1. Cyprus-Salamis (Acts 13:5)
2. Pisidian Antioch (Acts 13:14)
3. Iconium (Acts 14:1)

On the second trip, he repeated this pattern in these cities:

4. Thessalonica (Acts 17:1-2)
5. Berea (Acts 17:10)
6. Athens (Acts 17:17)
7. Corinth (Acts 18:4)
8. Ephesus (first pass) (Acts 18:19)

On the third trip, upon his return visit to Ephesus he repeated this strategy (Acts 19:8).

While many Jews were saved in these campaigns, interestingly, it was also an effective way of reaching Gentiles, as many God-fearing Greeks (i.e., converts to the Jewish faith) came to faith in some of the above cities, namely:

1. Pisidian Antioch (Acts 13:43)
2. Iconium (Acts 14:1)
3. Thessalonica (Acts 17:4)
4. Berea (Acts 17:12)
5. Corinth (Acts 18:7)

In this regard, this synagogue strategy served to pluck some of the low-hanging Gentile fruit among the Jews, since such people were already predisposed in their hearts toward God.

Second, Paul would employ as "Jew first, *then* Gentile" approach. While going to the synagogue was Paul's custom (Acts 17:2), it was not his endgame; in six of the eight cities he went to (as enumerated below), persecution broke out against his ministry:

1. Pisidian Antioch (Acts 13:45-46)
2. Iconium (Acts (Acts 14:2, 4-6)
3. Thessalonica (Acts 17:5-9)
4. Berea (Acts 17:13-14)
5. Corinth (Acts 18:6)
6. Ephesus (Acts 19:9, 23-41)

When this happened, having fulfilled his duty to preach to the Jews first, Paul would use these circumstances to then preach to the Gentiles. In Pisidian Antioch, this pivot resulted in explosive results as "many ... believed" and "the word of the Lord was being spread through the whole region" (Acts 13:48-49). In Corinth, as God steadied Paul's heart, many were brought to the Lord (Acts 18:9-10). In Ephesus, during Paul's two-year tenure, many Greeks became Christians (Acts 19:10). In Salamis and Athens, Paul did not face persecution from the Jews, but after visiting the synagogue, he proceeded to minister to the Greeks directly, with notable salvations seen (Acts 13:6-12; 17:34). The progression and outcomes of Paul's strategy by these two first methods can be summarized as follows (Figure 10.1).

Incredibly, this chart (Figure 10.1) shows Gentiles were saved in every city in which Paul employed the "synagogue first" method or "Jew first, then Gentile" strategy (per second and fourth columns, respectively). Gentiles were won either by hearing the gospel while attending Paul's synagogue meetings or through Paul's evangelism efforts outside of the synagogue.

Synagogue First Strategy	God-Fearing Greeks Saved?	Persecution by Jews?	Pivot to Gentiles (2nd Strategy) Salvations Seen?
1st Tour			
1. Salamis-Cyrus	–	–	Yes / Yes
2. Pisidian-Antioch	Yes	Yes	Yes / Yes
3. Iconium	Yes	Yes	–
2nd Tour			
4. Thessalonica	Yes	Yes	–
5. Berea	Yes	Yes	–
6. Athens	–	–	Yes / Yes
7. Corinth	Yes	Yes	Yes / Yes
3rd Tour			
8. Ephesus	–	Yes	Yes / Yes

FIGURE 10.1
Summary of Paul's results from his first two outreach strategies.

Third, Paul used a "Gentiles-only" approach in cities where there were no synagogues, as in Lystra, Derbe, and Philippi. In these situations, Paul looked for public places where he perceived there would be an openness to the gospel (Acts 14:8-10, 20-21; 16:13). In all three cases, this led to great outcomes. In Lystra, while preaching, Paul healed a lame man. When the multitudes saw this miracle, they proceeded to worship Paul and Barnabas as if they were the Greek gods Zeus and Hermes (Acts 14:11-18). In Derbe, "many disciples were made" as they responded to Paul's preaching (Acts 14:21). In Philippi, God opened the heart of Lydia, a God-fearer and seller of purple fabrics, which led to the church being planted (Acts 16:14-15, 40). In total, when using these three overarching methods, Paul saw Gentiles saved in all eleven cities he visited.

PAUL'S CREATIVITY—TWELVE EVANGELISTIC STRATEGIES

From this profile of success, there is a picture that emerges regarding Paul's creativity. Recall there was no template for Paul to follow in reaching a city. When he and Barnabas were first sent out, he had never planted a church. While he had been a vital part of the Antioch church, yet that work was established by the Cyprian and Cyrenian brothers, along with Barnabas' oversight (Acts 11:20-23). Paul did not start that work. So as Paul went out he had to learn on the job. Barnabas, his dear friend, was along with him during the first planting tour and most certainly provided some mentoring moments, but it was their prayerful dependence on the Holy Spirit that taught them how to plant effectively as Jewish brothers in new Gentile fields. In this regard, God helped Paul become a "situational genius." Drilling down further into Paul's strategies, we see his evangelistic creativity at work as each city provided a new opportunity or variation on the theme with which to reach out. Twelve different evangelism approaches can be delineated.

1. Confrontational evangelism: Elymas struck blind in Cyprus (Salamis) (Acts 13:10).
2. Crusade evangelism: Whole city turning out in Pisidian Antioch (Acts 13:44, 48-49).

3. Signs and wonders evangelism: Lame man stands to his feet in Iconium and Lystra (Acts 14:2; 14:10).
4. Suffering evangelism: Paul gets stoned in Lystra (Acts 14:9).
5. Intercessory evangelism: Paul looking to pray in Philippi (Acts 16:13).
6. Renewal or synagogue evangelism: Paul presenting "new wine" to Jews, the status quo faith community in Thessalonica (Acts 17:1).
7. Bible study evangelism: Eager ones were examining the Scriptures daily in Berea (Acts 17:11).
8. Apologetics evangelism: Reasoning with Epicurean and Stoic philosophers; preaching at the Areopagus in Athens (Acts 17:17-19, 22).
9. Tent making evangelism: Paul evangelizing and working as a tentmaker in Corinth (Acts 18:3-4).
10. Home evangelism: Paul used Titius Justus' home as an outreach base in Corinth (Acts 18:7). (Other additional house church references: Philemon's house church (1:2); Priscilla and Aquila's house church (Rom. 16:5,1 Cor. 16:19); Nympha's house church (Col. 4:15); Lydia's house church (Acts 16:14).
11. Lecture evangelism: Paul relocates to the public hall of Tyrannus in Ephesus (Acts 19:9). This hall also represents a religiously neutral place to do evangelism, which is defined as a location "not used for religious purposes" (Ugo, 2012, p. 6). Coffee shops, schools, civic halls, and hotels would be contemporary examples.
12. Discipleship-school evangelism: Paul teaching for extended periods in Ephesus (Acts 19:9-10).

From this list, we can see the variety of imaginative, practical, and supernatural ways Paul reached out. He was flexible, sensitive to the spiritual climate of a locale, and broke into new territories accordingly.

PHILIPPIAN EXAMPLE

As a window into Paul's innovative thinking, the Philippian story provides a helpful case study. Having just been beckoned there by the Macedonian vision, he must have wondered what God would have in store. How would Paul crack the code in reaching the city? Acts 16:12-13 tells us this:

We were staying in this city for some days. And on the Sabbath day we went outside the gate to a riverside, where we were supposing that there would be a place of prayer; and we sat down and began speaking to the women who had assembled.

Several things are instructive here.

One, Paul stayed in the city for "some days" prior to making a move. This represented Paul getting to know the lay of the land, gauging the spiritual climate, and getting his feet on the ground. This may have involved walking around the city, getting to know its geography, finding where the business district was, observing how people went about their day. This time was about creating a scouting report of the city. This was gathering natural intelligence for spiritual purposes.

Second, he was looking to pray. Just as Antioch built into him the primacy of prayer and worship, so he would pray and worship in every city he went to. From these times of prayer, wisdom would flow and love for the people would come from the presence of God. He would get God's heart for the city as he interceded for the city in the city. Intercession is praying on-site with insight.

Third, in looking to pray, Paul was also looking for like-minded people. Although there was no synagogue in Philippi, yet he looked to see if there were any who observed the Sabbath, as small a group as that might be. He would not be afraid of finding just a tiny group (Zech. 4:10). If he could find like-minded people, this would be a way to accelerate his learning about the city.

Note: Starting a synagogue required ten Jewish adults. This is referred to as *minyan* and the Jews based this numerical starting point on the picture given in Ps. 82:1 and the ten spies in Num. 13. That there were not even ten believing adults in the whole city was surprising since Philippi was a leading Roman colony and a leading city of Macedonia. This situation was telling of the spiritual condition in the city.

Fourth, Paul was not afraid to go "outside the gate" of the city walls. He was not afraid to do something unique or different as the Holy Spirit gave peace. He was adventurous and willing to try new things He could think outside the box.

Fifth, he was socially engaging. He initiated conversation with people by the riverside, in this case with the women who were gathered there.

He showed himself friendly and approachable. Every outreach must begin with a warm heart and firm handshake, or possibly a hug or peck on the cheek, depending on the cultural norm. The way to a city is through the heart of a person.

Sixth, God used their small, obedient steps to create a divine appointment. Lydia, a worshiper of God, was there by the riverside and overheard Paul's conversation. As God opened her heart, she not only came to faith, but her entire household came to faith as well (Acts 16:14-15). They were immediately baptized, and Paul and his team were able to start their church plant right then and there. This Philippian story showcases the kind of creative Spirit-led evangelism that Paul pioneered in city after city. Paul was ingenious, innovative, and bold, and it lead to great outcomes.

ACTIVATION—CREATIVITY (#7)

1. Describe the last time you did something novel and creative in your ministry. What were the results? How did people react?
2. Have you ever considered that the Father, Jesus, and the Holy Spirit are creative? Pick a story in the Bible to illustrate how this is true.
3. How do you stimulate new thinking in your life?

11

Key #8—Coordination: Infrastructure for This Plant

"You give them something to eat" (Matt. 14:16).

Every church plant must have those responsible for operations and administration—those who set the stage, prep the chairs, tend the soundboard, welcome the guests, count the offering, respond to emails, create graphics, and more. In time, processes and procedures will be needed, and systems and infrastructure must be put in place. Vision and mission give expression to logistics.

Jesus' primary "ops team" was His twelve disciples. Jesus tasked Judas to take care of the ministry books and assist in mercy ministries (John 12:6; 13:29). Philip was to take care of conference meals (John 6:5-7). The Twelve were sent as advance teams to towns Jesus would visit (Luke 10:1). They would be assigned to baptizing believers (John 4:2). They provided crowd control during Jesus' healing crusades (Mark 5:24, 31). They procured food for their ministry trips (John 4:31-33). Peter was in charge of income taxes (Matt. 17:24-27). Peter also offered to make special conference booths for Moses and Elijah as visiting guests (Mark 9:5). Two unnamed disciples were in charge of Jesus' entry into Jerusalem and preparing the donkey mount (Luke 19:29-35). Peter and John were in charge of details for the Last Supper (Luke 22:7-13). Peter served as security duty in Gethsemane, having lopped off Malchus's ear (John 18:10). John was executer of Jesus' will and appointed as guardian of Jesus' mother (John 19:26-27).

There are a thousand details that come with ministry. While administration and operations people may not get the glory of preachers and teachers, their role is no less important. As 1 Corinthians 12 teaches, all parts of the body are "indispensable" (v. 22). They provide invaluable assistance in making sure tasks are completed and that the ministry is run well.

As team leader, Jesus had a management responsibility: it was putting the right people in the right places. It was about getting people involved and having them own the mission. He trained the Twelve so they would later empower others to get involved when it was their turn to lead.

Jesus understood the value of those who took care of the what, where, when, and how. Jesus was not only spiritually minded, He was also grounded in the practical here and now. An integral part of church planting is setting up the infrastructure and coordination needed to make good on the ministry goals God has given.

PAUL: HARNESSING *KYBERNESIS* AND *PROISTEMI*

"God has appointed in the church ... [administrators]" (1 Cor. 12:28).

Paul had great insight into the realm of administration (*kybernesis*) and operations (*proistemi*), as given in 1 Corinthians 12:27-31 and Romans 12:3-8. The inclusion of these two gifts in the given passages indicate their importance in seeing a church function properly.

With regard to the gift of administration (Rom. 12:8), there are several points to highlight. First, those with the gift of administration are set in teams, in particular, working with "helpers" as given by the context of the verse. They are not working in isolation but in group settings. This means personal skills, institutional goals, and attention to details are all part of the administrator's field of operation. They are responsible for moving things along, getting things done, and marshaling resources to accomplish tasks (financial, physical, human). Second, administrators work with the main leaders in the church—namely, apostles, prophets, and teachers (1 Cor. 12:28a), which means they must have the trust of leadership, understand the DNA of the church, and represent the heart and spirit of the church as they go about their duties. They are there to help execute the mission of the church as articulated by senior leadership. Third, administrators are spiritually mature, as their ministry also works with those moving in the power gifts of healing and miracles. They assist in the practical matters of "delivering" the supernatural to the people.

Paul also talks about the grace of leading (*proistemi*: to rule, maintain, be over) in Romans 12:3-8. Here, we have an amplification of how operations work in the church. First, those with the gift of leading value the other gifts that are around them—for example, prophecy, serving, exhorting (Rom. 12:6-8). They understand that wisdom comes from the counsel of many viewpoints and perspectives (Prov. 15:22). Second, there are different levels of leading. According to a grace given to a person, one could lead a team of three people and one could lead a group of a hundred. Each person has their own measure and capacity (Rom. 12:6). Third, the grace which God gives to lead can express itself in different areas, such as leading in tech areas or small groups or worship ministry. Each person with the grace of leading has his or her own burden and focus. Fourth, this gracing has a strong work ethic, doing things with earnestness, care, and efficiency. Because of this gracing's propensity to be on task, it can be impatient with those who are less efficient. This provides an area of character development for those with this gift.

From these two passages, we see Paul's appreciation for administration and operations and how these gifts are essential to planting and growing a church. Coordinating the multitude of activities that come with establishing a church is not easy, and God has specifically gifted people in the body to assist with this. Look for those who can be administrators and coordinators.

ACTIVATION—COORDINATION (#8)

1. Have you built an "ops team" before? If so, describe for what purpose. How did the team perform?
2. What are your strengths and weakness in overseeing an administrative team?
3. When you think about operations for a church plant, list up to ten areas where you need help.
4. Have you taken a team through a scaling process? If so, describe what they had to grow into. What were the pain points?

Phase III

Disruption (Global Impact)

12

Key #9 — Commitment: Getting the Job Done

"When the days were approaching, He resolutely set His face to go to Jerusalem" (Luke 9:51).

There can be no kingdom advancement, no church planted, unless there is a fierce commitment to follow-through and execution. Seeing a mission accomplished takes determination and grit, and there are more than enough obstacles along the way for planters to want to quit.

The hassles of ministry can be demotivating and demoralizing. When the disciples failed in their healing prayers for an epileptic, Jesus said, "How long am I to bear with you?" (Matt. 17:17). When the Pharisees kept harassing Jesus with their incessant questions and opposition, Jesus responded with deep sighs (Mark 8:12), and later had to castigate them for their hypocrisy (Matt. 23). The people of Nazareth exhibited such detachment at Jesus' miracles that He "wondered at their unbelief" (Mark 6:6). The disciples' "hearts were hardened" despite witnessing the feeding of the five thousand (Mark 6:52). These kinds of things can wear on planters and cause them to think twice about what they signed up for. But this would only be par for the course.

When Jesus went to Jerusalem for the last time, He knew it would require a new level of fortitude; thus, the Scriptures say, "He resolutely set his face towards Jerusalem" (Luke 9:51). When Jesus considered the magnitude of dying on the cross, He was so exercised over the prospect, He asked the Father, if possible, for the cup to pass from Him (Mark 14:36). Being a finisher is no easy task, not to mention all the steps in between.

Hebrew 3 gives us a powerful and inspiring look at Jesus' commitment to His mission. The writer contrasts Jesus' assignment with Moses'. Moses was faithful "as a servant," while Jesus was faithful "as a Son" (Heb. 3:5-6). Moses delivered the people from Egypt; Jesus delivered the people from sin

(Gal. 1:4; Rom. 7:23-25). Moses gave the Law; Jesus fulfilled it (Matt. 5:17; Rom. 8:3-4). Moses was a five-star prophet-leader, yet he submitted his ministry to Jesus (Matt. 17:3, 5). Moses made great intercession for his nation, but Jesus lives to ever make intercession for all peoples (Ex. 32:11-4; Heb. 7:25). Moses labored as a loving shepherd, while Jesus is the Great Shepherd (Ex. 18:18; Heb. 13:20). Moses built the tabernacle; Jesus founded the church (Mt. 16:18). Rightly then, does the writer declare that Jesus "has been counted worthy of more glory than Moses" (Heb. 3:3). What Moses accomplished was staggering, yet incredibly, Jesus did infinitely more.

That's why He is called the chief Apostle (Heb. 3:1). Apostles accomplish the mission. They complete the task. They get the job done. It was Paul who would later observe, "The signs of a true apostle [are] performed among you with all *perseverance*, by signs and wonders and miracles" (2 Cor. 12:12). There can be no doubting Jesus was the greatest signs, wonders, and miracles guy to ever live. But less noticed is the mark of perseverance required of apostles. They follow through to the end (2 Tim. 4:7). Like Eleazar, one of David's mighty men who "stood his ground and struck down the Philistines till his hand grew tired and froze to the sword" (2 Sam. 23:10), apostles "hold on to the sword" until the victory has been won. Exiting is not an option.

The goal to make something happen is always easy until it's attempted. There is no dream that is not met with resistance, delays, disappointments, failure, obstacles, warfare—literally or figuratively—and even death. The commitment to execute, push through, and overcome is the acid test of how much a leader truly cares. Jesus was the ultimate finisher and accomplished a task like none other (John 17:4).

PAUL: DETERMINATION

> "I labored even more than all of them, yet not I, but the grace of God with me" (1 Cor. 15:10).

In comparison to the original twelve apostles, Paul had a checkered past since he was "a blasphemer and a persecutor and a violent aggressor" against the church (1 Tim. 1:13). Instead of being allied with the Twelve, he was initially their great opposer. As such he started out "in the hole" and considered himself to be "least of the apostles" (1 Cor. 15:9). This gave Paul extra motivation to prove himself as worthy of the call and to ensure God's grace toward him was not in vain (1 Cor. 15:10a). He would be determined and committed at all costs, and we see this expressed in many ways throughout his life.

PAUL THE ACHIEVER

When the Holy Spirit said, "Set apart for me Barnabas and Saul for the *work* to which I've called them" (Acts 13:2), the Greek sense for "work" contains the idea of achievement or deed (*evrgon*) (Johnson, n.d. p. 3). This indicates the mind-set Barnabas and Paul possessed when they were commissioned. They readied themselves mentally and emotionally. They were called to be achieve. They dialed into strength right from the start, and it served them well as their first church planting trip would be fraught with difficulty (e.g., Acts 14:19). But their determination paid off handsomely as God used them mightily through preaching and the performing of miracles (e.g., Acts 13:49; 14:3).

PAUL THE PERSEVERER

Later, while writing to the Corinthians, Paul had to reluctantly recite his own credentials ("toot his own horn"), noting that he was doing so "in foolishness" because he had to get his point across (2 Cor. 11:16-17). The leaders in the church seemed to have devalued Paul in consideration of other apostles, so Paul was put in the uncomfortable position of having to defend himself (2 Cor. 11:4-6). His foolishness was to cite his own spiritual résumé of what he had done in the Lord. What follows—quoted in full—is a wild picture of the stature of the man. It illustrates the perseverance and commitment that he walked in. Had he not been forced into itemizing his "exploits," there would be no record of all that he accomplished.

"But in whatever respect anyone else is bold—I speak in foolishness—I am just as bold myself. Are they Hebrews? So am I. Are they Israelites? So am I. Are they descendants of Abraham? So am I. Are they servants of Christ?—I speak as if insane—I more so; in far more labors, in far more imprisonments, beaten times without number, often in danger of death. Five times I received from the Jews thirty-nine lashes. Three times I was beaten with rods, once I was stoned, three times I was shipwrecked, a night and a day I have spent in the deep. I have been on frequent journeys, in dangers from rivers, dangers from robbers, dangers from my countrymen, dangers from the Gentiles, dangers in the city, dangers in the wilderness, dangers on the sea, dangers among false brethren; I have been in labor and hardship through many sleepless nights, in hunger and thirst, often without food, in cold and exposure. Apart from such external things, there is the daily pressure on me of concern for all the churches. Who is weak without my being weak? Who is led into sin without my intense concern? If I have to boast, I will boast of what pertains to my weakness. The God and Father of the Lord Jesus, He who is blessed forever, knows that I am not lying. In Damascus the ethnarch under Aretas the king was guarding the city of the Damascenes in order to seize me, and I was let down in a basket through a window in the wall, and so escaped his hands." (2 Cor. 11:21-33)

Could a portrayal be more compelling of a man committed to his call? While every phrase could be highlighted, is it not astonishing (to pick out a few) that Paul was "beaten without number" (he lost count?); five times he received thirty-nine lashings; and then this little detail, "often without food" (he struggled at times to even have his bare essentials met?). Truly, it was fitting for Paul to share in 2 Cor. 6:4-10:

But in everything commending ourselves as servants of God, in much endurance, in afflictions, in hardships, in distresses, in beatings, in imprisonments, in tumults, in labors, in sleeplessness, in hunger, in purity, in knowledge, in patience, in kindness, in the Holy Spirit, in genuine love, in the word of truth, in the power of God; by the weapons of righteousness for the right hand and the left, by glory and dishonor, by evil report and good report; regarded as deceivers and yet true; as unknown yet well-known, as dying yet behold, we live; as punished yet not put to death, as sorrowful yet always rejoicing, as poor yet making many rich, as having nothing yet possessing all things.

Nothing more needs to be said about Paul's commitment. He could not and would not be defeated.

PAUL THE FINISHER

Given the above discussion, it's not surprising that Paul was able to say in his last days, "I have fought the good fight, I have finished the course, I have kept the faith" (2 Tim. 4:7). Like Jesus, Paul was the ultimate finisher, and in that, both men provide a definitive picture of what is required of the church planter. Impact can't come unless there is a complete commitment to execute on the mission. Planters get the job done.

ACTIVATION—COMMITMENT (#9)

1. Share three "war stories" you've been through in pursuit of your ministry goals.
2. Share a "regret" story of when you failed to deliver on a promise. What did you learn from it?
3. Please list five things you've accomplished in your life that illustrate your determination, whether it's natural or spiritual.

13

Key #10—Coin: Faith for Finances

"Seek first His kingdom and His righteousness, and all these things will be added unto you" (Matt. 6:33).

Incredibly, there is no record of Jesus ever making a fundraising pitch in His ministry. This doesn't mean He didn't do it or was unaware of the financial burdens of starting and sustaining a ministry; it's just that the Gospels don't speak to it.

Indeed, it can be inferred that Jesus supported not only Himself but also the twelve disciples whom He called to be with Him (Mark 3:13-14; note "their support" in Luke 8:3). Thus, His financial responsibility was high, having to sustain a team for three years as the disciples traveled with Him full time. He had to cover their expenses for food, shelter, travel, clothing, and most likely the needs of the disciples' families during this period, as the apostles-to-be left behind their professions (Matt. 4:19-22). It's possible the Twelve drew on their personal savings to keep their households going while they were away, which would have helped defray costs for Jesus, but nevertheless, it was a huge financial undertaking for Jesus to mobilize His team. Jesus also had His own mother and siblings to worry about—particularly, as the oldest son—although the burden may have been lightened by the family's carpentry business. Nevertheless, the question remains how did Jesus provide for His church planting initiative?

A conversation with Peter about taxes provides an informative look into how Jesus did it. In the midst of their hectic ministry, Peter was asked by revenue agents whether Jesus paid the "two-drachma tax" (Matt. 17:24). Speaking for Jesus, Peter responded in the affirmative, and in a conversation shortly thereafter, Jesus told Peter how the taxes were to be paid. Peter was to "go to the sea and throw in a hook, and take the first fish that comes up; and when you open its mouth, you will find a shekel. Take that and give it to them for you and Me" (Matt. 17:27). Sure enough, the first fish Peter landed contained the money they needed to pay for both their dues. (To state the obvious, Jesus was a great boss.)

This is a fascinating story full of insight into how kingdom financing works.

First, it could not have been lost on Peter that the financial provision came from a fishing expedition. When Jesus first called Peter, He said, in a play on words regarding Peter's natural vocation, "Follow me and I will make you fishers of men" (Matt. 4:19). By finding the coin in the fish's mouth, Jesus was giving Peter a memorable object lesson about the will of God. When one walks in God's calling, the provision will always be there. God's will is God's bill. God's supply for our daily and earthly needs will always be provided for when we obey Him. The pursuit of spiritual goals does not exempt us from our earthly responsibilities. Paying taxes, though a man-made concept (Matt. 17:25-26), is nevertheless to be honored, so as to not cause the world to stumble. When we seek first His kingdom, "[everything] will be added unto us" (Matt. 6:33). We can rest in faith. We need not fear. If the Father provides for the birds of the air and adorns the lilies of the valley with His glory, how much more will God provide for us (Matt. 6:25-30)? Jesus was in complete rest about His ministry finances. *Faith was His fundraising technique.* He did not have to raise money in the traditional sense (although there's nothing wrong with doing so; see below); it's just that His faith was so deeply rooted and His trust in the Father so real, He knew God's storehouse would be open.

Second, God's provision is designed to be supernatural so He gets the glory while our faith for the mission is strengthened by the miraculous supply. How crazy was it that a fish contained money in its mouth, and that the first fish that Peter caught would be the right one with the right amount of money? What were the chances? Did this not echo the manna that supernaturally appeared in the desert morning by morning? (Ex. 16:4, 13-21). Did not this echo the water that came from the rock at Rephidim? (Ex. 17:1-7). Did this not echo the plundering of the Egyptians when Israel was released by Pharaoh? The Hebrews went from slaves without a penny to having their bank accounts filled (Ex. 11:1-2; 21:35-36). To be sure God provides by natural means too, but His trademark is providing supernaturally.

Third, part of God's supernatural provision is it comes from unexpected places. A fish's mouth? Manna from the sky? Water from a rock? Many times, planters will lock in on a picture of how they think God will provide. But God owns the cattle on a thousand hills (Ps. 50:10). He can provide in any way and as creatively as He wants. Often God surprises us with provision from the most unlikely of places. (See our testimony in Chapter 2 of the Mini-Book; atheist realtor sells home to pastor and loses double commission on purpose.)

Fourth, God's provision is always right on time. Jesus' taxes were not overdue. He was not in arrears. It may have been close to the deadline, but Jesus did not sweat where the money would come from. He knew God would provide. This picture of rest was not a one-time example. This is was Jesus' normal state. He knew all the bills would be paid according to schedule. This was a matter of kingdom witness. Christians are to be financially trustworthy.

Through this story, we see how Jesus was spiritual and practical at the same time. He needed finances to carry out his ministry. There were real obligations to be taken care of. How would he meet the needs of the ministry? Faith was His foundation, which then unlocked real-time, real-life provision. Faith unlocks heaven's treasury for our earthly needs.

Then there is another snapshot of how God releases kingdom finances through ministry partners. As Jesus was going about from one city and village to another, proclaiming and preaching the kingdom" (Luke 8:1), the Scripture says there were many willing supporters of His ministry: "Joanna the wife of Chuza, Herod's steward, and Susanna, and many others who were contributing to their support out of their private means" (Luke 8:3). These givers were part of Jesus' extended ministry team, and they even itinerated with Him (Luke 8:2). This shows the faithfulness and goodness of God, in that He will open the heart of supporters to be "constant companions" so the team can focus on the spiritual mission, while they, as backers, focus on the financial needs of the ministry.

This passage also gives an important insight into the bond between the spiritual workers and financial suppliers. Part of the joy for partners is seeing the fruit of what happens through their dollars. When they can see firsthand—as Mary, Joanna, and Susanna did through their travels with Jesus—it increases their joy and makes them feel part of the work. The planters' mission gives the partners' gifts a real sense of meaning and purpose.

We also see these partners willingly gave to Jesus' efforts; as in Jesus did not have to implore them, beg them, guilt-trip them, or manipulate them to give. They saw the impact of what was going on, and their hearts were opened up to help. They *initiated* the supply line. As private donors, there were no committees or red tape to fight through to secure funds.

The donors were the direct gatekeepers, allowing for timely decisions and little delay. This made for greater efficiency in Jesus' ministry.

Among this support team, we see Joanna and Susanna served as "lead givers," along with other tiers of giving among the partners, no doubt in proportion to their ability (2 Cor. 8:3). It should be noted as well the role of women in driving kingdom advancement. Their financial contributions were crucial. Women have many roles in the kingdom, and this is another example of their strategic contribution to Great Commission work.

One note of caution in this discussion of finances: in most cases, going into the ministry is not an avenue for getting wealthy. However, when endeavors are greatly blessed like Jesus' was, money can pour in because of the excitement and momentum generated. Lean times can give way to surplus and bounty, and the temptation arises to use monies to personally enhance one's financial status or lifestyle. Jesus could have easily parlayed His influence into personal riches—more than anyone in history. Yet He did not do this. Despite countless opportunities to enhance himself, He always maintained a modesty and kingdom decorum that was befitting of the gospel. He never gave in to the love of money. In this, Jesus was a sharp counterpoint to the Pharisees who loved wealth (Luke 16:14). As professional clergy with institutional standing among the people, the Pharisees had access to a continuous flow of the people's offerings. Far from suffering, they were well taken care of and had ample finances for their retirement years. They loved the system they were in because of what it did for their bank accounts. As church planters, don't become corrupted by "much coin." Like Jesus, keep the main thing the main thing, and the secondary things the secondary things. Don't be torpedoed by riches if they come your way.

PAUL: GOD IS FAITHFUL

"I know how to get along with humble means, and I also know how to live in prosperity" (Phil. 4:12).

Paul's faith for finances can be described as a two-tiered system of support. His first and *primary tier* was to support himself (Siemens, 1997); this was his default mode (Acts 20:34; 18:3; 1 Cor. 9:6; 2 Thes. 3:8).

In keeping with his religious training, "Rabbis practiced a trade so as to be able to impart their teaching without charge" (Bruce, 1977, p. 220). Paul carried this habit over into his new role as an apostle. Paul's joy was to make the gospel free to his listeners (1 Cor. 9:18; 2 Cor. 11:7). Although he was deserving of support (1 Cor. 9:3-12; 1 Tim. 4:17-18; 2 Tim 2:6), he did not want people to think that his motives were anything but pure (1 Thess. 2:5, 10; Acts 20:33, 1 Cor. 9:12; 2 Cor. 2:17). He would even take pains to pay for his own food (2 Thes. 3:8). Why did Paul embrace such a model of self-support? As he told the Thessalonians, "not because we do not have the right to do this but in order to offer ourselves as a model for you, so that you would follow our example" (2 Thes. 3:9). Pursuant to being an example, Paul supported himself on his first planting tour (1 Cor. 9:6), while planting the church in Thessalonica (1 Thes. 2:9; 2 Thes. 3:8), as a tentmaker in Corinth (Acts 18:3; 1 Cor. 4:12), and while planting at Ephesus (Acts 20:34). He was a model of the self-financed planter.

Then, alternatively, as occasion would arise, he would accept un-solicited gifts. This was his *second tier* of support, his supplemental tier. While in Corinth, it can be inferred—since Paul stopped working—that Silas and Timothy brought funds from the Macedonian brothers and sisters (Acts 18:5). In this case, he received it with gratefulness and took it as God's provision to be able to fully focus on planting. Paul speaks directly about this time when he later wrote to the Corinthians, "I robbed other churches by taking wages from them to serve you; and when I was present with you and was in need, I was not a burden to anyone, for when the brethren came from Macedonia, they fully supplied my need" (2 Cor. 11:8-9).

With regard to the "brethren that came from Macedonia," this was in reference to the beautiful example of the Philippian church and the support they provided for Paul's ministry (Ogereau, 2014). As Paul writes of their financial gifts,

> You yourselves also know, Philippians, that at the first preaching of the gospel, after I left Macedonia, no church shared with me in the matter of giving and receiving but you alone; for even in Thessalonica you sent a gift more than once for my needs. Not that I seek the gift itself, but I seek for the profit which increases to your account. But I have received

everything in full and have an abundance; I am amply supplied, having received from Epaphroditus what you have sent, a fragrant aroma, an acceptable sacrifice, well-pleasing to God. (Phil. 4:16-19)

Paul considered their gifts as "participation in the gospel from the first day until now" (Phil. 1:5) and was so encouraged by their thoughtfulness, he continually remembered them with thanksgiving in his prayers and rejoiced greatly over them in the Lord (Phil. 1:3-4; 4:10). The Philippians' connection to Paul as their founding father was strong, and as God prospered their congregation, which was populated with successful business people, they were anxious to help Paul (Phil. 4:10).

For Paul, depending on the situation, "in any and every circumstance," he knew how to abound in lean times and prosperous times. He knew the "secret of being filled and going hungry, both of having abundance and suffering need" (Phil. 4:12). He was content to work, and he was content to be aided by offerings. His default was to support himself, but he also welcomed outside help.

This articulation of Paul's approach to finances is not to minimize or disqualify the donor development model in any way. Paul speaks of how apostles like Peter and others were supported in this way through generous churches and individuals (1 Cor. 9:3-6). Yet for Paul, the grace that worked in him called him to not utilize any of these rights (1 Cor. 9:15). His reward was that, "when I preach the gospel, I may offer the gospel without charge, so as to not make full use of my right in the gospel" (1 Cor. 9:18). Such was Paul's joyous faith in this matter of money.

ACTIVATION—COIN (#10)

1. Describe two situations when God provided for your finances in a supernatural way.
2. What is your view of church planting while tentmaking? Is it favorable, neutral, or negative? Explain why.
3. First, Timothy 6:10 speaks of those who have "pierced themselves with many griefs" because of their love for money and chasing after

it. Have you ever fallen victim to scams or get-rich-quick schemes? If so, please share.

4. Tithing is the foundation of proper financial management. Do you tithe on your income? If so, for how long have you done this?

14

Key #11—Constancy: Protecting the Plant from Diversions

Jesus said to Peter, "Get behind Me, Satan!" (Matt. 16:23).

There is nothing the devil would like more than for a church plant to get off track. The church is the most potent organization in the world and the greatest threat to the kingdom of darkness, so the Enemy constantly seeks to defend his hold over cities against any planting efforts.

Because of Jesus' status as the cornerstone of the Church (Eph. 2:20), to divert Jesus would have been to divert the birth of the church. Or to put it starkly, to divert Jesus was to abort the church. Thus, Jesus had the burden of protecting the church before it was even born. As Jesus went about establishing the church, there were various attempts to derail Him.

First, we see how the devil came to tempt Jesus in the desert (Matt. 4:1-11). These were not the typical disqualifying temptations thrown at men. The devil didn't tempt Jesus with the "big three"—sex, money, and power (girls, gold, glory); instead, his attack was at a much higher level. He attempted to recreate the garden scene when Adam fell. When Adam and Eve committed the first sin, it was because the serpent succeeded in appealing to their flesh ("good for food"), their eyes ("delight to the eyes"), and their pride ("the tree was desirable to make one wise") (Gen. 3:6). This is what the apostle John refers to as the lust of the flesh, lust of the eyes, and the boastful pride of life (1 John 2:15-16). When the devil tempted Jesus to turn the stones into bread (appealing to the flesh, Matt. 4:3), to throw Himself off the pinnacle of the temple that the Father might rescue Him (appealing to pride, Matt. 4:6-7), and to bow down to the devil upon seeing the glories of the world (appealing to the eyes, Matt. 4:8-9), the devil was tempting Jesus in the exact same threefold manner as he did with Adam and Eve. But note the scenery change. When

Adam and Eve fell, creation became cursed (Gen. 3:17-19), and Jesus now stood in the wasteland where the garden once was. The desert represented the devil's victory over man. If it worked on the first Adam, then it would surely work on the second Adam. But the devil's attempt to disqualify Jesus failed. The devil's preemptive strike on Jesus' ministry in its early stages didn't work. Jesus was too strong.

Second, the religious system as represented by the Pharisees and Sadducees was constantly opposing Jesus and tried to undermine or outright destroy Jesus' message. Jesus came to preach a new covenant, a new people, and the message of grace. The leaders would have nothing to do with it. They were incensed by Jesus' healing on the Sabbath. They were incensed by His association with sinners and tax collectors. They were incensed by His disregard for the temple. Under such pressure, Jesus could have moderated His language and taken the edge off of His teachings. He could have compromised and accommodated the leaders and their traditions, but He did none of this. To do so would have been to dilute the gospel. The message had to stay pure. Jesus would never forsake what the Father told Him. God's agenda would not be edited or mutated by man.

Third, the people were so taken by Jesus' ministry that they wanted to make Him king (John 6:15). He would be their answer to tyrannical Roman rule. He would be the answer to the dry and lifeless leadership of the Pharisees and Sadducees. His love for people, His compassion, His understanding, His boldness—it was just what the people wanted and needed. They wanted Him to usher in a new era of leadership. John the Baptist had previously taken the nation by storm and the people thought he might be the Christ, only to be stunned by the greater glory of Jesus (Luke 3:15-16). But the people didn't understand they needed a Suffering Servant, not a conquering king. They didn't realize they needed a Lamb who would take away the sins of the world. They didn't realize the temple sacrifices, as sacred as they were, were just a fore-shadowing of the ultimate sacrifice that would be given. Jesus re-presented God's *kairos* timing to reconcile the world to God; enjoying God's everlasting reign of righteousness, peace, and joy would come later. Jesus never wavered from the divine sequence of this agenda. He would not allow the temporal adulation and adoration of the people to sway Him or tempt Him to be king before His mission of the Cross was first fulfilled.

Fourth, we see Peter, Jesus' appointed disciple to lead the church, trying to stop Jesus from going to the cross (Matt. 16:22). As well-intentioned as Peter might have been, he did not realize the church couldn't be established without Calvary. Seizing on this lack of understanding, the devil personally took it upon himself to work through Peter's ignorance. Therefore, in no uncertain terms, Jesus had to rebuke Peter, "Get behind Me, Satan!" (Matt. 16:23). Jesus had to be strong and blunt despite His love for Peter and the friendship they shared.

Fifth, Jesus' siblings and mother tried to "rescue Him from Himself." The revival triggered by Jesus' ministry was unprecedented. Everywhere He went He was swarmed and mobbed. People were coming from all parts of the country to hear and see Him do miracles. There was hardly a moment to rest. His family, not understanding God's sovereign purposes at work, took umbrage at this and decided they needed to intervene. States Mark 3:20-21, "[Jesus] came home, and the crowd gathered again, to such an extent that they could not even eat a meal. When His own people heard of this, they went out to take custody of Him; for they were saying, 'He has lost His senses.' In Matthew's account, we are given Jesus' response to this "intervention":

> While He was still speaking to the crowds, behold, His mother and brothers were standing outside, seeking to speak to Him. Someone said to Him, "Behold, Your mother and Your brothers are standing outside seeking to speak to You." But Jesus answered the one who was telling Him and said, "Who is My mother and who are My brothers?" And stretching out His hand toward His disciples, He said, "Behold My mother and My brothers! For whoever does the will of My Father who is in heaven, he is My brother and sister and mother." (Matt. 12:46-50)

To rebuff one's own mother (and brothers and sisters) was a bold thing to do, but this is what Jesus did. Family loyalties could not be above Jesus' allegiance to the Father (Mark 10:28-30). Like Peter, as well-intentioned as His family might have been, they did not understand the call and what was at stake. Jesus would not be pushed off-center, even by His own family.

Sixth, Jesus could have gotten caught up with His own ministry success. With national fame and popularity surging, Jesus could have been taken with the euphoria sweeping the country. Like superstar athletes or singers, His schedule could have been taken with endless invitations and requests for appearances. But Jesus never forgot His priority to be with the Father. He never forgot the simple discipline of having His "quiet time." In fact, this would be His refuge. His continual dependence on the Father served to keep Him in perfect alignment. He would not fall victim to busyness. He protected His church planting efforts by making sure to take care of Himself spiritually. This is why He overturned the tables in the temple and stated emphatically that the house of God must be a house of prayer. If prayer loses its centrality in a planter's life (or any disciple's life), then his call can easily get off course.

Seventh, Jesus never wandered from His "base." Jesus loved all people (John 3:16), but especially the hurting, the lowly, the humble, the downcast, the distressed, the sinners, and the tax collectors (Luke 4:18-19; Matt. 9:36; 11:19). They would be His "people." Jesus didn't come to spend time with the those who were healthy but those who were sick (Luke 5:31). His picture of a good day was to give hope to the hopeless. Even up to the last moments before He died, Jesus ministered faithfully to those in need; a thief's request for mercy would not be denied (Luke 23:43). As God revealed to Moses how He was compassionate, gracious, slow to anger, and abounding in loving-kindness and truth (Ex. 34:6), in like manner Jesus would show Himself thus to the contrite and brokenhearted. He never lost His focus on the tending to the sheep He was sent to comfort (Mt. 11:5).

PAUL: APOSTOLIC SHEPHERD

"I am amazed that you are so quickly deserting Him who called you by the grace of Christ, for a different gospel; which is really not another ... . If we, or an angel from heaven, should preach to you a gospel contrary to what you received, he is to be accursed!" (Gal. 1:6-7, 9).

STAYING ON MESSAGE

The message of grace was not to be tampered with. To do so would be to incur Paul's wrath—even curses (Gal. 1:9). Why such ferocity on the part of the apostle? Simply because lives were hanging in the balance. The only way to salvation was through Jesus Christ (John 14:6). Said Paul to Timothy, "It is a trustworthy statement, deserving full acceptance, that Christ Jesus came into the world to save sinners" (1 Tim. 1:15). No one else has or can do this. Salvation is by grace through faith (Eph. 2:8-9). This is what the Reformers would codify into the Five Solas (*Sola Scriptura, Sola Fide, Sola Gratia, Sola Christo, Soli Deo Gloria*). No implication or hint of human work (legalism, karma, indulgences, asceticism) could be applied towards salvation. The religions of the world pinned their hopes of eternity on doing good as a way to earn their way to heaven. This formulation was wrong in any and all forms.

When Adam fell, it would require a second Adam to rescue humanity out of its predicament. Just as sin entered the world through one man, so salvation would come through one man (Rom. 5:12, 15). Only one man's work would do because only one man could do it. And what a work it would be. Calvary would be the beginning of the turnaround and the message by which all who called on the name of the Lord would be saved (Acts 2:21; Rom. 10:13), Jew or Gentile (Rom. 1:16).

To deviate or veer off course from this pure message was to make a cataclysmic mistake, not just a little one. Paul would not allow any small leak to spring, lest the whole boat sink. He would not allow a fraction off plumb to appear, lest down the line the entire target is missed. This was not just a matter of individual concern; it was also a matter of ecclesial concern. The church's message would be in peril if people were allowed to embrace a mutated message. Additionally, with the church in its infancy—only fifty years out from the cross—this would have historical implications; the church had to be protected from careening off into a doctrinal ditch. The church had to stay on message at all costs.

Paul thus spoke with great authority. The threshold for triggering the protective anger of Paul on this issue was extremely low. Paul stood as an alert watchman. No contamination, virus, or "enemy on the horizon" would be allowed in the camp. In showing himself strong on this issue, he showed all planters where the red line was.

In a related doctrinal situation, Paul had to keep the church in Colossae (and its sister churches) on track with regard to the work and person of Jesus. No philosophy could take precedent over who Jesus was or what He did (Col. 2:4, 8, 16-23). This was a matter of orthodoxy. Stated Paul regarding Jesus:

He is the image of the invisible God, the firstborn of all creation. For by Him all things were created, both in the heavens and on earth, visible and invisible, whether thrones or dominions or rulers or authorities—all things have been created through Him and for Him. He is before all things, and in Him all things hold together. He is also head of the body, the church; and He is the beginning, the firstborn from the dead, so that He Himself will come to have first place in everything. For it was the Father's good pleasure for all the fullness to dwell in Him, and through Him to reconcile all things to Himself, having made peace through the blood of His cross; through Him, I say, whether things on earth or things in heaven." (Col. 1:15-20)

Or to sum up, "For in Him all the fullness of Deity dwells in bodily form, and in Him you have been made complete, and He is the head over all rule and authority" (Col. 2:10-11).

Paul's passion for the church to be the pillar of truth was evident in his letters both to the Galatians and to the Colossians. If the church didn't stay on message, who would? Be strong dear planters. Never waver in preaching and protecting the gospel.

STAYING PURE AND IN GOOD ORDER

Another challenge for Paul was represented by his two letters to the Corinthians. In those letters, he addressed a plethora of issues—from divisions to morality, to Christian liberty, to use of the gifts, to the settled fact of the resurrection, to offerings, and more. These letters represent the labor of love involved in planting—not to dissimilar to herding cats, a nearly impossible task. Yet, helping a new congregation to mature is about training them to act in a way that reflects kingdom culture. This takes time and patience. "Children will be children," and raising a church requires the love of a parent (1 Thes. 2:7, 11). Doesn't it seem like common sense to not eat your own meal first before taking communion (1 Cor. 11:20-22)? Doesn't it seem like common sense to not talk over each other when someone else is prophesying (1 Cor. 14:31)? Doesn't courtesy demand you don't use your own freedom to cause another brother to stumble (1 Cor. 8:9)? The answers may seem obvious in retrospect, but not obvious to those starting out at living in a manner worthy of the gospel of Christ" (Phil. 1:27; 1 Thes. 2:12). Keeping a church in good order and moving it toward maturity is hard work.

Of note in the Corinthian situation was an incident regarding incest. This was a dire moral situation that had to be corrected, but the church lacked urgency in addressing the issue (1 Cor. 5:1-5). As Eph. 5:3 states, "immorality or any impurity or greed must not even be named among you," let alone a sin of this magnitude. The moral standard of the church had to be upheld. The bride of Christ is to be without spot or wrinkle, holy and blameless (Eph. 5:27), and this situation was definitely a stain that needed to be removed. Paul used his authority to bring the necessary cleansing (1 Cor. 5:5).

STAYING OUTWARD-FOCUSED

Jesus said to the church, "Let your light shine before men in such a way that they may see your good works and glorify your Father who is in heaven" (Matt. 5:16). It's human nature once we find a comfort zone to stay there. We find family. We find friendship. We find good teaching. We find safety. We find identity. These are great things, and part of the blessing in being part of God's family. However, this comfort also can lull people to a place where they lose their outward focus on reaching the lost, serving the city, and ministering to the hurting. In writing to Timothy and Titus, Paul made clear to not allow the church to drift or get soft in this regard. The church must be "zealous for good deeds" (Titus 2:14) and "learn to engage in good deeds to meet pressing needs, so that they will not be unfruitful" (Titus 3:14). Good works in a person's life are a sign of maturity, and helps them stay other-focused (1 Tim. 5:10, 6:18). Planters are tasked to help new works maintain a servant mindset and stay on track with regard to being God's redeeming presence in their communities.

ACTIVATION—CONSTANCY (#11)

1. Name three tough decisions you've made to stay true to your mission.
2. Have you ever offended anyone because of staying true to your convictions? If so, what was the conviction? Was it worth it? If so, why?

3. Name three examples that illustrate your ability to prioritize and keep distractions out on an organizational level (not personal level).

4. Write down examples in which you allowed your organization to go sideways. Which tendency outweighs the other in your life as a leader? Staying on track or getting distracted?

15

Key #12—Continuation: Raising Up the New Disruptors

"Go therefore and make disciples of all the nations" (Matt. 28:19).

JUST AS JESUS TAUGHT THEM

Luke's second volume—the book of Acts—provides the ultimate commentary on whether Jesus' strategy to focus on training the Twelve proved to be the right move. Would they establish His church? Would they pass on His teachings? Would they become fishers of men? Would they exhibit His anointing and power? Would they exhibit His care and love? Would they walk in purity and consecration? Would they remain humble and authentic? Would they be prayer warriors? Would they love one another as Jesus loved them? Would they seek to glorify the Father in all things? Would they lay down their lives for the cause if necessary?

The record answers yes to each of these questions. Jesus was so successful in discipling the Twelve that the church exploded with excitement, growth, and vitality. In short order, just ten days after Jesus' ascension, on the day of Pentecost, the church was officially "incorporated." Having committed themselves to prayer, just as Jesus taught them (Matt. 6:5-15; 18:18-20; 26:36-46), the apostles received the Holy Spirit's promised power and the effect was immediate.

Peter preached with such authority that three thousand people came to faith that morning, and a mass baptism ensued (Acts 2:41). All of a sudden, their training in handling crowds under Jesus came in handy. There was joy and gladness in the air (Acts 2:46). The believers were moved to share their goods and property with each other, to the point they had "all things in common" (Acts 2:44). The apostles preached the Word and performed healings just as Jesus taught them (Matt. 10:1-8,

Luke 9:1-2), and as a result, God "was adding to their number day by day those who were being saved" (Acts 2:47).

The religious leaders were quick to retaliate, but Peter and John stood their ground. They could not stop speaking of what they had seen and heard (Acts 4:20). Their obligation was to obey God rather than men (Acts 5:29). They were doing just what Jesus had modeled for them (Matt. 22:16; Luke 12:4-5). They counted it a privilege to be "considered worthy to suffer shame for Jesus' name" (Acts 5:41), just as they were taught in the Sermon on the Mount (Matt. 5:10-12).

Their call to be fishers of men proved to be truer than they could have ever imagined. After the initial three thousand were baptized, another five thousand were saved (Acts 4:4). Then with more miracles flowing from the apostles, "all the more believers in the Lord, multitudes of men and women, were constantly added to their number" (Acts 5:14). And without an end in sight, "the word of God kept on spreading; and the number of disciples continued to increase greatly in Jerusalem, and a great many of priests were becoming obedient to the faith" (Acts 6:7). They had caught more "people" than they did fish in all their years as fishermen.

By this time, as the gospel saturated all of Jerusalem, the apostles' training was in full bloom. All that Jesus had poured into them, they were now pouring into the newly birthed church. The multiplier effect was overwhelming. Jesus' strategy to invest in the Twelve was more than validated. No doubt, Jesus, looking down from heaven was proud of His disciples.

One other leadership event is worth highlighting; i.e., the apostle's decision-making process as a team. As previously noted, the apostles had decided that circumcision was not necessary for salvation. To render this decision, they had to grapple with such questions as, "Was circumcision a vestige of the old covenant or was it to be carried over into the new covenant?" "Was circumcision a uniquely Jewish mark or was it to be incorporated by all peoples to have saving faith?" Interestingly and significantly, it was James and not one of the main apostles who provided the clarifying principle on the issue (Acts 15:13-18). For the apostles to hear the Lord through James showed their humility and mutual submission one to another; they did not feel the "final decision" had to come from them. Just as Jesus taught them, they walked in humbleness (Mark 10:42-45).

Additionally, part of the final decision was undergirded by Peter's encounter with Cornelius, who was a Gentile. That Peter recognized God was granting repentance to those who were "unclean" helped the brethren to see the message of grace at another depth (Acts 10:28; 11:18). Jesus' work at the cross was a finished work. No extra works would be needed. Their affirmation showed great courage and inspiration. Despite their Jewish heritage, they let go of one of the most sacred aspects of the Old Testament and opened the door for all nations to come to faith through an unencumbered gospel. They moved in unity and their spirit of unity and brotherhood was a great glory to God.

IT WORKED OUT JUST AS PLANNED

As gifted as Jesus was, His goal was never to be a one-man show. His plan was bigger, longer, and more far-reaching. His mission would not die with him or leave when He ascended into heaven. In some regards, his mission was to instill the mission in others. It was to pass on the beauty of what the Father had given him. Continuity would be crucial. Succession would be essential. DNA transference was strategic. In pursuit of that, outside of his death on the cross, *Jesus' organizational wisdom to focus on his top lieutenants was pure genius.* It was about raising up the new disruptors. The true measure of a dream is whether it's bigger than the man. World change must be generational. It must beget legacy and continuation. After Jesus' death, there was no interruption. The transition was flawless, and the church flourished greatly. Everything worked out just as Jesus planned it.

PAUL: RELEASING NEW APOSTLES

"You therefore, my son, be strong in the grace that is in Christ Jesus" (2 Tim. 2:1).

PAUL THE MULTIPLIER

Paul was tireless in his training of next-generation disciples and leaders. It's been calculated that he worked in close proximity with nearly one hundred people over the course of his ministry (Murray, 1998, p. 190). This not to mention the multitude of people he won to the Lord or taught in some kind of classroom or Christian education setting as found in Antioch and Ephesus (Acts 11:26; 19:9-10). He was a man who was exceedingly fruitful.

Of particular interest in the movement from conception to construction to disruption is the all-important final step—that of raising up successors. Moses had Joshua. Elijah had Elisha. David had Solomon. Jesus had the Twelve. In many ways, this is the litmus test of organizational strength. Have successors been raised up to continue the work with like conviction and care? In this regard, we see Paul succeeded greatly in this manner.

Paul mentored Silas, Timothy, and Titus (Chapter 8). He mentored Epaphras (Chapter 9). He mentored Priscilla and Aquila during their tentmaking days in Corinth (Acts 18:2). Some have also suggested the contingent which accompanied Paul in Acts 20:4 were also all young apostles trained by Paul (Porta, 2013). In this case, another seven men would have been raised up by Paul to become part of a new wave of leaders that would carry on his church planting tradition.

A HEART TO RAISE UP SUCCESSORS

From these examples, we see that Paul understood the importance of continuation. In his last letter—written to Timothy—Paul stated his time of departure was near (2 Tim. 4:6). Fittingly, his last letter was written to his beloved son in the Lord, one with whom he had worked closely, poured his heart into, and remembered with great fondness. If there was anyone who understood Paul, it was Timothy. Said Paul to his mentee,

> You followed my teaching, conduct, purpose, faith, patience, love, perseverance, persecutions, and sufferings, such as happened to me at

Antioch, at Iconium and at Lystra; what persecutions I endured, and out of them all the Lord rescued me! ... Continue in the things you have learned and become convinced of, knowing from whom you have learned them. (2 Tim. 3:10-11, 14)

Retain the standard of sound words which you have heard from me, in the faith and love which are in Christ Jesus. Guard, through the Holy Spirit who dwells in us, the treasure which has been entrusted to you. (2 Tim. 1:13-14)

This Timothy is the one of which Paul told the Philippians, "You know of his proven worth, that he served with me in the furtherance of the gospel like a child serving his father" (Phil. 2:20-22). In wanting to pass on his best to Timothy, Paul gave him this exhortation: "You therefore, my son, be strong in the grace that is in Christ Jesus. The things which you have heard from me in the presence of many witnesses, entrust these to faithful men who will be able to teach others also" (2 Tim. 2:1-2).

Verses 1 and 2 are intimately tied together. Verse 2 speaks of Paul's fourfold picture of succession: Paul (first generation) to Timothy (second generation), to faithful men (third generation), to others who can also teach others (fourth generation). Continuation would be a four-generation prospect, taking up to a hundred years to fulfill. This is a vision that would have longevity. But the key to this process would be grace (verse 1). This was Paul's foundation: "By the grace of God I am what I am" (1 Cor. 15:10). He knew if Timothy and the succeeding generation of leaders could be apprehended by the grace of God as he had been, then the enterprise of the church would be in good hands. The mandate to raise up successors would be fulfilled, and organizational effectiveness would continue in the same Spirit, joy, and power that Paul experienced.

ACTIVATION—CONTINUATION (#12)

1. Write down a list of five to six characteristics that are most important to you in a successor. Keep a list of potential candidates. Observe them over time to see which one progresses best according to your list.

2. Have you ever succeeded someone? What was that experience like for you (good or bad)? What lessons will you apply when it's your turn to appoint a successor?
3. Describe three people who you have raised up as leaders. For what position? What were some keys you learned in training up these people?
4. If you die today, who will lead your organization? How are you preparing your successor?

Conclusion

16

Canvas: Jesus' Model of Impact—Church Unleashed

The examples left to us by Jesus and Paul are inspiring and instructive. That Jesus could so naturally and so powerfully showcase his organizational acumen is worthy of praise. Paul, following in the footsteps of Jesus, punctuated how powerful Jesus' church planting principles were and the impact that results from following them. Could there be any better teachers?

THE PLANTER'S LEADERSHIP CANVAS—TABLE, MATRIX, AND TOOLBOX

To summarize and crystallize the lessons in this book, the twelve keys from the life of Jesus are placed in a planter's leadership canvas as provided below (Table 16.1). It can be seen variously as a table, a 3 × 4 matrix, or a toolbox, depending on how you want to use it. It's a table if you want to have an overview of Jesus' impact model. It's a 3 × 4 matrix if you want to break it down into leadership modules. It's a toolbox if you want a picture of how to plant a church. Alternatively, it could be used as a diagnostic for consulting, or as a coach's checklist for encouraging a planter (or pastor). In any of these cases, an organizational framework is provided by which a class, a training curriculum, or a boot camp can be created to expand on topics related to each of the respective twelve areas in Jesus' Model of Impact.

For example, in quadrant 3 (*Capability*), the following materials could be added:

- Homiletics class
- Counseling skills
- Change management

TABLE 16.1

Planter's Leadership Canvas

JESUS' MODEL OF IMPACT
12 LEADERSHIP KEYS FOR CHURCH PLANTING

CONCEPTION	CONSTRUCTION	DISRUPTION
LEADER	**NEW PLANT**	**GLOBAL IMPACT**
1. CARING DEEPLY The call of God. Luke 2:49 - "I must be about My Father's business." **Paul: APPREHENDED FOR CHRIST** Acts 26:19 - "I did not prove disobedient to the heavenly vision." BE ON FIRE	**5. CORE TEAM:** Finding those who will plant with me. Luke 6:13 - "He called His disciples to Himself and chose twelve of them." **Paul: ASSEMBLING TALENT** Acts 16:3 - "He took Timothy." BE A RECRUITER	**9. COMMITMENT:** Getting the job done. Luke 9:51 - "He resolutely set His face to go to Jerusalem." **Paul: DETERMINATION** 1 Cor. 15:10 - "I labored even more than all of them." BE GRITTY & POSSESSED
(MISSION)	*(MOBILIZATION)*	*(EXECUTION)*
2. CLARITY Caring deeply must have a compelling, tangible goal. Luke 19:10 - "I came to seek & save the lost." **Paul: CALLED TO THE GENTILES** Acts 9:15 - "He is a chosen instrument to bear my Name before the Gentiles." BE A VISIONARY	**6. CULTURE** How will this this plant work, look, and feel? MaZ. 16:18 - "I will build my church." **Paul: INSPIRED ARCHITECT** 1 Cor. 3:10 - "Like a wise master builder, I laid a foundation." BUILD KINGDOM ATMOSPHERE	**10. COIN:** Faith for finances. MaZ. 6:33 - "Seek first His kingdom and all these things shall be added unto you." **Paul: GOD IS FAITHFUL** Phil. 4:12 - "To get along with humble means and ... to live in prosperity." BE FAITH-FILLED
(ARTICULATION)	*(ORG DESIGN)*	*(PROVISION)*
3. CAPABILITY Planting must be connected to skill, especially preaching. Luke 4:18 - "The Spirit of the Lord is upon Me." **Paul: EQUIPPED & QUALIFIED** Acts 22:3 - "I [was] educated under Gamaliel." BE GOOD AT WHAT YOU DO	**7. CREATIVITY:** Planting with genius. John 2:9 - "The headwaiter tasted the water which had become wine." **Paul: NEW THINKING** Acts 16:13 - "And on the Sabbath day we went outside the gate." BE IMAGINATIVE	**11. CONSTANCY:** Protecting the plant from diversions. MaZ. 16:23 - Jesus said to Peter, "Get behind Me, Satan." **Paul: APOSTOLIC SHEPHERD** Gal. 1:6 - "I am amazed that you are so quickly deserting Him for a different gospel." BE UNCOMPROMISING
(CREDIBILITY)	*(INNOVATION)*	*(CORE VALUES)*
4. CONSECRATION The key to your plant. John 14:10 - "I am in the Father, and the Father is in Me." **Paul: INNER LIFE** Col. 3:3 - "For you have died and your life is hidden with Christ." BE STRONG IN SPIRIT & IN TRUTH	**8. COORDINATION:** Infrastructure for this plant. MaZ. 14:16 - "You give them something to eat." **Paul: KYBERNESIS & PROISTEMI** 1 Cor. 12:28 - "God has appointed in the church...[administrators]." BE AN ADMINISTRATOR	**12. CONTINUATION:** Raising up the new disruptors. MaZ. 28:19 - "Go therefore and make disciples of all nations." **Paul: RELEASING NEW APOSTLES** 2 Tim. 2:1 - "Be strong in the grace that is in Christ Jesus." BE A MULTIPLIER
(SP. AUTHORITY)	*(OPS & ADMIN)*	*(SUCCESSION)*
PERSONAL ARENA BUILDING UP YOURSELF	ORGANIZATIONAL ARENA BUILDING UP YOUR TEAM	GLOBAL ARENA MAKING A DIFFERENCE

Or in quadrant 8 (*Coordination*), the following topics could be addressed:

- Building a finance team
- Implementing ministry software
- Establishing a volunteer training course

Note that each quadrant has a blue vertical tag associated with it (e.g., "ORG DESIGN" for box 6, *Culture*). This is meant to expand the canvas as a teaching tool by associating each quadrant with a related **LEADER-SHIP SPHERE** to be mastered. In box 6, the attribute of *Culture* speaks to the larger domain of *organizational design*. In box 11, the attribute of *Constancy* connects to the larger sphere of *core values*.

Additionally, leadership **EXHORTATIONS** are given in blue capitalized phrases as a way to spur application. These sayings convey the leadership **IDENTITIES** planters should possess. It's a way to picture yourself at work. Thus, for box 9, the exhortation to "Be gritty and possessed" relates to EXECUTION and getting the job done, which connects back to *Commitment*. Box 5 exhorts one to "Be a recruiter," because planters are called to MOBILIZATION as they build their *Core Team*. Stated in active form, these imperatives represent the leadership behavior that must be embraced to become a successful planter.

CARRYING IT WITH YOU

As a way to further impress and personalize Jesus' organizational wisdom upon our minds, a key chain diagram is provided below (Figure 16.1). This restates the idea that caring deeply provides the unifying conviction behind what is done. As put forth in this book, there is a distinct inside-out progression. It begins inside the planter and then works its way out to actual planting. The layers of the key chain are engraved with the principles contained in Jesus' Model of Impact; they are to be faithfully assimilated so that it's like having them in our pocket—on call, on demand, and always ready to be used. Master these and you will be empowered in your planting leadership.

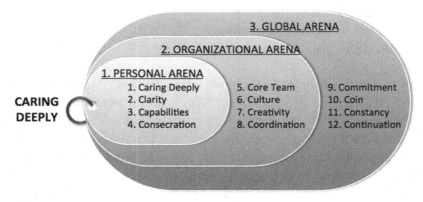

FIGURE 16.1
Key Chain of Progression for Planters

ACTIVATING THE CANVAS AND KEY CHAIN

1. Pick three blue exhortations in the canvas and share how they speak to you as a planter.
2. List three to five subjects you'd like to teach under each of these twelve headings in the canvas.
3. Memorize the twelve elements of Jesus' Model of Impact in the key chain.

17

Final Challenge: Paul, Apostle of Love

THE LOVE OF PAUL'S LIFE WAS JESUS CHRIST

Jesus said he who is forgiven much loves much (Luke 7:47) and for Paul, this saying was deeply personal. Paul's early life was marked by education, religious fervency, and a desire to excel. Paul distinguished himself as a Jew of Jews (Phil. 3:5-6). Yet despite Paul's towering intellect and his vaunted role as a teacher of the Torah, none of this prepared him for the arrival of Jesus. Not only was Paul unreceptive to the Son of God, but he was also a violent aggressor against Jesus. Intent on snuffing out all threats to the Law, Saul helped lead the charge in persecuting the new Jesus followers to the point of presiding over Stephen's stoning (Acts 8:1-3).

It was this persecuting spirit that made Paul so objectionable that he would write to Timothy in his later years that he was chief among sinners (1 Tim. 1:15).

But God's mercy was greater. He who hated much would soon love much. Having set Paul apart from his mother's womb, God would orchestrate a dramatic conversion of the great persecutor (Gal. 1:15; Acts 9:1-9). Paul would taste firsthand the profound grace of God.

Due to his blinding encounter with Jesus, Paul experienced a blackout period of three days, in which he neither ate nor drank—a period that led to his salvation (Acts 9:5, 9-18). Shortly thereafter, and to the astonishment of everyone, he immediately "began to proclaim Jesus in the synagogues, saying, 'He is the Son of God'" (Acts 9:20). The Scripture testifies that "all those hearing him continued to be amazed, and were saying, 'Is this not he who in Jerusalem destroyed those who called on this name, and who had come here for the purpose of bringing them bound before the chief priests?'" (Acts 9:21). But the more Paul preached

Jesus, the more he grew. Acts 9:22 says that he "kept increasing in strength and confounding the Jews who lived at Damascus by proving that this Jesus is the Christ."

Paul became a powerful preacher of faith, hope, and love, with love being the greatest (1 Cor. 13:13). There would be no doctrine above the love of God. Love surpasses knowledge (Eph. 3:19). The goal of our instruction is love (1 Tim. 1:5). We can never be separated from the love of God (Rom. 8:38-39). Love is the fulfillment of the law (Rom. 13:10). Let all things be done in love (1 Cor. 16:14). The love of God controls us (2 Cor. 5:14). Faith must work through love (Gal. 5:6). Put on love (Col. 3:14). Be rooted and grounded in love (Eph. 3:17). "Abound in love, just as we do for you" (1 Thess. 3:12). "May the Lord direct our hearts into the love of God" (2 Thes. 3:5). God has given us a spirit of love (2 Tim. 1:7). We are nothing if we don't have love (1 Cor. 13:1-3). Love never fails (1 Cor. 13:8).

Whilst Paul is commonly revered for his masterful teachings, yet at the root, he was an apostle of love. Spreading the knowledge of Jesus through planting local churches was his passion and call. Never mind that he did this in an era when there were no trains, planes, internet, video, radio, TV; only dusty roads, boats, and donkeys. His accomplishments were otherworldly because he loved greatly. He left an indelible mark because he cared deeply.

This is what this book is about—helping you to become the best church planter you can be by identifying the organizational disciplines that flow out of care. There is no organization more important than the local church. She is the apple of God's eye. But it all starts with love. Dear church planter: *Is Jesus the love of your life?*

18

Coda: God's Glory Rests on the Church

In this book, I've laid out an organizational pattern given to us by Jesus. Why does God give us a pattern to follow? Because it takes out the guesswork, brings clarity, and gives confidence that we are doing the right things in the right way. It's how God releases His wisdom to us. In the Old Testament, we see this prominently featured when God gave meticulous instructions to Moses on how to build the tabernacle that would travel with the Israelites as they journeyed in the wilderness (Ex. 25:9; Num. 8:4). "See that you make them after the pattern ... which was shown to you on the mountain" (Ex. 25:9; Heb. 8:5).

More than one-quarter of the book of Exodus (eleven chapters) is fully devoted to every detail of how to build the tabernacle—down to the materials, colors, and dimensions; from the use of ram skins, acacia wood, and gold overlays, to how to make the ark, the lampstands, and the sockets for the pillars. These instructions were followed scrupulously by Moses (Ex. 39:32), and at the dedication of the tabernacle, the Scripture describes the following outcome: "The cloud covered the tent of meeting, and the glory of the LORD filled the tabernacle. Moses was not able to enter the tent of meeting because the cloud had settled on it, and the glory of the LORD filled the tabernacle" (Ex. 40:34-35).

Later, when Solomon established the first permanent temple, he too faithfully followed the pattern as given by God to his father David (1 Chron. 28:11-12, 19). Upon completion, like Moses, Solomon experienced the same glory when the temple was dedicated:

> When the priests came forth from the holy place ... the house of the LORD was filled with a cloud, so that the priests could not stand to minister because of the cloud, for the glory of the LORD filled the house of God. (2 Chron. 5:11, 13-14)

Two for two.

Fast-forward to the New Testament, and we see the glory poured out a third time on the temple (Acts 2); except, in this case, God's temple was the church, the people of God (Eph. 2:19-22; 1 Peter 2:5). It was here that the Holy Spirit came with power and might just as Jesus promised (Acts 1:8).

The fact that the visible manifestation of God's glory was associated with His temple in three dispensations signals how important the temple is to God, with the Church being His final expression. Thus, in looking to plant churches, we are pursuing a goal of the highest kind—how to build a temple upon which God so readily pours out His glory. King David said, "O LORD, I love the habitation of Your house and the place where Your glory dwells" (Ps. 26:8). This is the point of our obsession— spreading His glory through planting new works. Let our churches be little or big dots of lights that cover every corner of the globe.

Mini-Book

Five Stones Church: Our Start-Up Story and a Little Beyond

Introduction

This mini-book at the back of the book is a summary of how we started our church in the beautiful city of Vancouver, BC. God led us here in 2003 after twelve years of pastoring in Minneapolis, Minnesota, where I led a wonderful church that sent missionaries around the world and served as a hub for twenty-plus other sister churches in the Midwest. This is where I got my start in the ministry after switching from a research career in the medical sciences.

The subsequent shift from pastoring to church planting, while sudden, came naturally given the strong missional environment I came from. We landed on Vancouver because of its cosmopolitan vibe, reputation as one of the most livable cities in the world, and its position as an international gateway city to Asia (I was already ministering to leaders in that region).

Our research of Vancouver and of Canadian culture at large told us it would not be an easy assignment. Canada was well into a postmodern ethos, and Vancouver in specific had already proven refractory to many ministries that tried to get established. I told my American friends that Canada was much more like Europe than the United States. That's how they needed to think about its spiritual climate.

Our impulse to go to Vancouver was not based on an invitation from an existing church or a group looking for leadership. We went out of a burden that we were called to plant a church in a global city, that our natural passion for dynamic metropolises led us to this, and that God was pointing the way. This venture would be a start-up from scratch. Indeed, because of immigration policies, we couldn't bring a core team. It would just be our family riding on my wife's Canadian citizenship that would allow us to move to Vancouver in July 2003.

What follows are some of the lessons we learned as we planted. Variously, I think of this little book as having several titles:

- *A Short Book about Building Great Things*
- *17 Keys to Building a High-Impact Church*

- *Planting Big Churches in Small Spaces on Purpose*
- *Growing Your Church to Under 10,000 People*
- *Stories from the Front Lines with an Ocean View*
- *Microsize Churches in Megasize Cities*

Of course, these lessons are meant to accentuate and reinforce the organizational model given in this book. I trust it will add some sparkle and color to what you've already read.

Chapter 1—Miracles: Breaking the Barrier of Six

A new plant begins when God puts a burden in the heart of a planter to make a difference in a city. The mission of impact begins with God as He looks to extend the grace of His government through human vessels. Once the call is issued and accepted, the assignment is about living a life of faith and adventure from that point on. Every step requires trust in God, and whether it's discerned or not, every answer and provision that comes from those steps is a miracle.

When God called our family—my wife, Memie, and our four children, Kimmie, Heidi, Holly, and Matt (at that time twelve, ten, eight, and five years of age)—from a wonderful church of six hundred people to go to Vancouver, it was a scary but exciting time. Having taken the first step to transplant our family, we were now faced with the reality of finding like-minded people who would want to be part of a new beginning. Where would they come from? How would we connect? Where would we begin? Never mind breaking the barrier of fifty, one hundred, two hundred, or a thousand people, we had to break the barrier of six!

Of course, the church planting manuals are full of great tips for connecting and starting out, and we took those advices to heart—spreading the word, sending out mailers, setting up Starbucks appointments—but the results still had to come from God. The journey of trust was starting. We weren't just talking about church planting any more, we had to do it. So off we went, filled with prayer, excitement, and due diligence.

Then it happened.

I was at my new bank making a deposit when the teller noticed that my pen had a Christian saying on it.

"Are you a Christian?"

"Yes, I moved here to start a church."

Then, seemingly in slow motion, the question came, "Can I come to *your* church?"

There it was. Our first inquirer, the first person who asked about coming to "our church." Someone was asking about our dreams. My answer was an excited yes, but inside it was, "Yes, yes, a thousand yeses. God, I can't believe you're doing this. It's actually happening."

The teller and her family showed up at our first meeting.

We had broken the barrier of six.

The feeling was like the rush of having one's first baby (or close to it!).

That first miracle, seeing the substance of our faith materialize, became a lesson of *first principles*. In this venture of starting a church, we would have to always trust God's hand to be at work every step of the way.

Chapter 2—Faith Markers: God Did What?

Planters need faith markers so when dark days or debilitating doubts become overwhelming, they can look back and know God is with them. It gives the planter the strength to press through and carry on.

When we began our fundraising to go to Vancouver, we raised three years of support in three days.

When we put our house on the market, it sold in four hours at full price.

When we bid on our house in Vancouver, the transaction was handled by an atheist realtor who later told us, "When I saw you guys, I knew right away you were supposed to have this house." Little did we know that he would cause an existing deal for the house to collapse so we could purchase it. And by doing that, he gave up a double commission because he was representing the buyer and the seller.

Finding a good school for our four kids was a big priority. We researched diligently to find the right one, but when the first day of classes rolled around we seemed to have made the wrong choice; something seemed off right from the start. We decided immediately to look for alternatives. On a Wednesday morning of the same week, we submitted our kids' names to another school but it had a two-year waitlist. Wednesday afternoon we got a call asking for the ages of our kids. Upon hearing our response, the admissions person said a missionary family had just left the school that had the same number of kids with the exact same ages as ours! They said to submit our applications as soon as possible since the school year had already started. By Friday morning our applications were in and by the following Monday, the kids were enrolled in a new school that had a two-year waitlist. Wow. Having our kids settled in a new school in a new country while starting a church meant the world to us. All our kids stayed at this school until they graduated from high school.

A year after our move, I felt God telling me to shut down a ministry software company I had founded. I had started it as a backup plan to our support raising, thinking it could provide income for us in the future if needed. But managing it took a lot of my time, and the sense came to close it down even though I had invested a good chunk of money into it. I wrestled back and forth with God for several days before finally giving it up. A week later, a donor provided an additional year's worth of support with one check. The donor had no idea what I had done with my business.

There are other stories to be told, but these examples were crucial faith moments reassuring us that we were in God's will. God loves to get behind us supernaturally and to ensure we have all the confidence we need to face future challenges. He knows how to fortify us.

Chapter 3 — Flywheel: Throwing Two-Yard Passes

Don't get into church planting if you're not up for hard work and long hours with little praise. Church planting is not for the faint of heart. One study found that being a pastor-church planter is one of the five most stressful jobs a person could have (up there with air traffic controller and hospital administrator). This is due in part to the hundreds of things that need to be tended to in the starting stages—from preaching to setting up chairs, printing the bulletins, brewing the coffee, stringing up banners, negotiating rental contracts, loading up the truck, and turning out the lights. Now, repeat that a hundred times.

I call this "throwing two-yard passes." The task in itself may seem small, but its significance is huge. We all want to get into the end zone. We all want to score a touchdown (using an American football analogy). We all want to see souls saved. We want to see the church grow. We want to see people get baptized. This is what church planters live for. But not every play results in a score. You need to "drive down the field." A run here, a pass there—sometimes you don't make the first down and have to come off the field. But still, you go back on to the field so you can score. The process of doing a myriad of little things over a sustained course of time is what business author Jim Collins (2001) calls the "flywheel." It's the accumulation of a thousand small contributions of effort and re-petition that lead to a breakthrough moment. You barely know how and why it happens, except that when the shift comes, you look back and see how each little turn of the wheel led to more and more momentum until a breakout season happens.

The Bible refers to this as sowing and reaping, and it says that in due time we will reap if we do not grow weary in well doing (Gal. 6:9).

Church planting will certainly yield touchdowns, but it takes throwing a lot of two-yard passes. If you don't like being in the trenches, if you have a history of being lazy and taking shortcuts, then you are not the right fit for being a planter. You shouldn't do it. But if you can see the mundane as divine and the significance of the little then you will have the joy to labor in the day of small beginnings.

Chapter 4—Excellence: Pint-Size Churches with Keg-Size Taste

The apostle Paul never planted a big church by modern standards. All his churches were small yet packed with power and flavor—the flavor of the gospel and the person of Jesus Christ. Just like a Skittles candy, which is the size of a peanut but bursting with flavor, high-impact churches do not have to be big to change landscapes. They can be pint-size with keg-size taste.

Excellence is about what's on the inside. Quality in, quality out. A high-impact church by nature will be excellent—not because of its big budget or its largeness (although there's nothing wrong with either)—but because of its mind-set. Excellence is about the passion to do "all things well" (Mark 7:37).

You can have excellence whether you have a shoestring budget or a million-dollar budget (we once raised $2,000 for families that couldn't buy Christmas gifts for their kids; our budget was $19). Having a million-dollar budget is no guarantee of quality (think of poorly made cars), just like having a $100 budget is no curse to having have a shoddy operation (think lemonade stands). It's not about the physical assets, it's about the mindset, a desire to excel no matter the circumstances.

If there's no passion for excelling then cheap comes out.

Think of the warm chocolate chip cookies made by your grandmother, or the $20 Swiss Army pocketknife or the $50,000 Mercedes-Benz. They are all examples of excellence. They are all champions in their category. But each has a cheap counterexample. There are bad-tasting chocolate chip cookies; there are poorly made $20 pocketknives, and there are $50,000 luxury cars you regret buying. The question is, why would anyone make a cheap version when it can be excellent? Aren't the excellent versions the ones that endure, become desirable go-to products, create customer loyalty, and even reach iconic status?

The reason things end up cheap is because the makers of cheap don't have an inner conviction. Someone making cheap chocolate cookies doesn't have the love of a Grandma. The maker of a cheap knife doesn't have a conviction about how an emotional bond can be created over something as practical as a multi-purpose pocket tool . The maker of junk cars think of them as only transportation from point A to point B, instead of a living space on wheels where great conversation, thinking, and interlude can occur. This is the difference between excellence and non-excellence. It's about translating deeply held care and conviction into reality.

As churches, we have the highest beauty to inspire us: Jesus Christ. Can there be anything more motivating and passion inducing? This is why excelling should flow from the church. The church should be using as much creativity, ingenuity, and affection as the best organizations out there. Excellence is inherently attractive, and thus inherently evangelistic. **You were attracted to Jesus because of His excellency, not because He was on discount.** This is the goal and passion of church planting. Do all things with quality. It's not about the size of the barrel, it's about the size of the taste.

Chapter 5—Personal Prayer Summits: Ascending the Mountain to Get Your Tablets

There is nothing like clarity. Moses had the heavy task of not only rescuing a nation, but also establishing it. How would he do that? He had never started a nation before. What would its constitution be? What would be the rules and norms for governing the Jewish people entrusted to him? God had called them to be a people set apart for Him; what would that look like?

Thankfully Moses didn't have to come up with his own ideas. God bid him to go up the mountain where after forty days God downloaded the divine plan and edicts to him. Its cornerstone would be the Ten Commandments.

Church planting is a small version of that. We are planting a "royal priesthood, a holy nation, a peculiar people" (1 Peter 2:9 KJV). But to do that, we need the clarity that comes from the mountain. We need to ascend the hill like Moses did. This is where personal prayer summits come in. As a planter, you must spend quality time on the mountain to get your tablets.

In the first three months of our plant, I felt a tug from God to embark on a consecrated season of prayer, modeled after Daniel's seeking of God three times a day (Dan. 6:10). For ninety-plus days I did this. The things that God spoke to me during this time were empowering, clarifying, and invigorating—all crystallized in the phrase "plant a big-church, small-church." I didn't get Ten Commandments like Moses did, but the one commandment I got was well enough. I was thrilled. This was the compass I needed to get going properly and not feel like I was running around with my head cut off. Time does not permit to detail all the particulars of what this one commandment meant, except to say it was tailored perfectly for the spiritual climate and culture in Vancouver.

People in this city were very suspicious of big churches. They were not into the big boxes they saw in the United States. In fact, they wanted to avoid the appearance of looking like a U.S. church. So all the stuff I learned from the States went out the window.

As I wrote in my diary: "The ground here is pan-hard. There is no Christian radio allowed in the city. The only Christian radio signal we get is from across the border in the United States, south of us by thirty miles. No new church construction permits have been issued in Vancouver proper in thirty-five years. The mayor of our suburb vowed not to allow a church to be built. Christmas advertising is not allowed in the malls."

So the strategy of "big-church, small-church" was to think big but personalize it by coming alongside people, make things relational, and win people's trust bit by bit. Overcoming their hesitation and skepticism of church was like trying to get someone back to a restaurant where they had had a bad meal. It's tough sledding. So presenting the gospel in a "small church" format was the way to go—but not compromising the big vision God had put in our hearts.

This all came from "the mountain" which was born from a season of consecrated prayer. This cycle would repeat itself several times in the first years of our plant (see next chapter). God had on-the-ground intelligence for us. We just needed to position ourselves to receive it. Every planter needs these mountaintop encounters to get God's wisdom and strategy. A nation, as Moses showed, depended on it.

Chapter 6—Blueprint: Have You Had Your Napkin Moment?

Many well-known businesses and big ideas have been conceived on a napkin—from Oprah's media empire to the font on our credit cards (Hines 2017).

In our second year, during another season of consecrated prayer, our entire church went on a forty-day fast, with people signing up for the days on which they would pray and give up meals. It turned out to be another turning point for our start-up, except this time we didn't get a tablet chiseled with one commandment, we got a whole blueprint.

While I was reading the story of David and Goliath, my eyes were suddenly opened to a new narrative. This was more than a "little guy defeats a big guy" story. It was actually an apostolic blueprint, a divine schema that itemized what it meant to plant churches, from terms of the battle to how to win the war. It was as if the heavens parted and shafts of light beamed down with insight and understanding. It was my "napkin moment." God was sitting with me and diagramming how it'd all work. It was so natural—like we were sitting at a kitchen table—and yet so profound. The template He gave became pivotal to us and provided the outline for building our church from that moment on. These insights became branded into our hearts and minds. They became part of our identity. Much of the teaching of Chapter 2, "Church Planting Is a Breakthrough Initiative," came from this time of fasting. Those insights and exhortations are still as fresh for us today as when God first gave them.

To add to what was shared in Chapter 2 of the main body of the book, there were some other key "napkin points" we received: (1) Goliath represents the big assignment planters face, so think big, dream big; big faith wins. (2) Creativity is a showstopper. When Goliath met David in battle, he was greatly surprised. His demeaning tone and words toward

David were in effect saying, "What is this? Who are you?" He did not anticipate going up against a shepherd boy. This was God's strategy at work. Creativity changes the convention of what is expected and creates gospel-centered surprises. It creates new associations and dispenses with the old. Creativity changes perceptions. Out of this insight, creativity became a huge rally cry for us at Five Stones, and part of what we would become known for in the future. (3) The youthfulness of David represents a perpetual freshness of the Spirit we are to possess. Churches should never become stodgy or stale, not matter how old the congregation is. (4) The "five" of David's five smooth stones (from which our church got its name) is the number of grace; it represents the gospel of grace. (5) Churches need to aim at becoming high achievers. Killing giants is a noble goal. (6) Churches also need to be good at finishing the job (as in cutting off Goliath's head). Don't let a job be half-done.

I believe God has a napkin moment for every planter. God loves to make us feel like geniuses.

Chapter 7—Megachurch Credibility: Creative Spaces

People love creative spaces. One of my new learning curves in planting the church was discovering how much a well-designed space can help people become more open to the gospel.

When we were faced with the choice of picking between a vacant vocational school and a one-hundred-year-old warehouse as our first full-time facility, we were caught between the practical (less expensive, more room) and the creative (more expensive, great heritage vibe). Some of our leaders wanted the school option, while others wanted the heritage spot. I was torn. My default would have been to go with the practical space (which included an allotment of free parking; a big plus in crowded Vancouver), but newly armed with the creative focus of our "napkin blueprint," we were pulled to go with the warehouse site even though it would cost us tens of thousands of dollars to spruce it up. The school was in move-in condition but the warehouse required renovating.

Ultimately, we decided on the warehouse (with a central downtown location) because it gave us the creative feel we were looking for. The building was outfitted with sturdy wood beams, wide-slatted flooring from the early 1900s, and iron-reinforced pillars. Because we had an architect-turned-pastor on staff (another miracle story for later), we were able to transform this old, dusty space into a beautiful fusion of heritage and modern. People were uniformly impressed. We had the city's Arts Council request that our spot be used as an official gallery. As reported in the local newspaper, one of the Arts Council directors, stated,

> Holy hell, did you hear about Five Stones Church? You should see this church! It was just a buzz of all buzzes. People all [said] to me, if the restoration of the old buildings in this city truly ended up resembling like what they've accomplished in that building, everyone in this entire city would be all for it. There would not be one single call to forget the past

and tear it down to build new because it is beyond stunning. (Fleming, 2011, p. 13)

We hosted a mini-fashion show because our environs provided a great backdrop. Films and TV directors began requesting use of our building (e.g., J. J. Abrams shot a pilot scene in our stairwell; the TV show *Property Brothers* used our space for taping their dialogue segments). Political campaigns were launched, nonprofit concerts were hosted, and mayor-sponsored city events were held. Not only did this building serve as our spiritual base, but it had become a resource for the whole city. In effect, we had megachurch credibility. Little did I realize, even though the largest area in our building could only accommodate a hundred people (where we had our Sunday services), we had a visibility and name that was much larger than our seating capacity. "Big-church, small-church," just like God said. Follow the "napkin plan" and see what He does. Great things come in small packages.

Chapter 8—Drop Your Nets: Doing the Work of an Evangelist

I've always said there were four kinds of church growth, but after coming to Vancouver, we found a fifth. We found an inordinate number of Christians that were on the sidelines, not going to church and out of the game. In many cases, these Christians had been unattached to a church for years. Then something would quicken them and they would feel the need to find a church again. So they would join a church not because they came from another church or just got saved, they were just coming in off the sidelines. Here then are the five kinds of church growth:

1. Transfer Growth—Church growth from members moving from one church to another.
2. Conversion Growth—Church growth from people getting saved.
3. Renewal Growth—Church growth from people shifting to a Spirit-filled experience.
4. Biological Growth—Church growth due to families having more kids.
5. Sideline Growth—Church growth due to reengagement and reconnection.

How were we to engage people from these varied backgrounds? How would we go about outreaching?

Evangelism is definitely a learned skill for me. It doesn't come naturally. Because I'm shy by nature I have to work at it. Yet Paul's word to Timothy has given me a lot of comfort: "Do the work of an evangelist" (2 Tim. 4:5)—as in, you don't have to *be* an evangelist, just do the *work* of one. Be diligent to do what evangelists do without having the burden to be gifted like one. You don't have to be a Billy Graham.

During our first three and a half years, here are some of the things we did to drop our nets:

- Billboard campaign ("Back to Church")
- Pro-hockey outreach with Adam Burt
- Newspaper advertisements
- Postcard mailings
- Movie outreaches (*Narnia, Passion of the Christ*)
- Acts of kindness (stress-relief gift bags)
- Free ESL classes
- Free Mandarin classes
- 100-minute Bible outreach
- Banquet evangelism (Easter, Christmas)
- Picnic events
- Seeker Bible studies
- College Bible study (Simon Fraser University)
- Evangelistic sermon series
- Meals for the homeless
- Clothing distribution
- Vacation Bible School
- Character camp
- Family gym nights
- Home meetings

I'm happy to report we were faithful in reaching out but sad to report we didn't catch nets full of fish. We did catch some but not by the boatloads. Conversion growth was not our mainstay, rather our increase came from renewal and sideline growth.

Chapter 9—It Feels Good Here: Work Hard at Setting the Atmosphere

Ephesians 2:2 says the devil is "the prince of power of the air." He is a master at creating atmospheres. This is in part how he controls and influences people. Atmosphere affects behavior—negatively or positively. This is what marketing is about: creating moods when you walk into stores so you'll buy.

But God is the originator of atmosphere and heaven is the best there is. In concert with this, the church is called to create great atmospheres since we're partners with God. I believe one of the calls of apostolic ministry is to set a dynamic kingdom environment.

Here are seven atmospheric qualities to consider:

1. *Create an atmosphere of encouragement.*
   Set a tone of affirmation and encouragement by how you talk and communicate, whether verbally or otherwise. Set a positive, faith-filled tone. Celebrate little victories. Acknowledge service from your members. Be proactive and authentic.
2. *Create an atmosphere of leadership.*
   There must be security in the air. One wise church planter said, when people come to church, they ask, "Who loves me, and who's in charge?" Lead with heart, with love, with vision, with care, with humor, with authenticity, and with authority. The world tries to erode authority, but authority is designed by God to bring safety, covering, and most importantly, life. Jesus said in John 14:6, "I am the way [leadership], the truth [wisdom], and the life [peace and joy]." Corporate happiness results from great leadership.
3. *Create an atmosphere of learning and insight.*
   People must be spiritually fed. This is the first principle of discipleship. Work hard at teaching and preaching well. Pray to get

God's burden each Sunday. Step into the pulpit with confidence and preparation. Learn to move and speak out of the anointing. Be in step with the Holy Spirit.

4. *Create an atmosphere of friendship and personal care.*

Ultimately, a pastor can only touch so many people. So small groups, ministry groups, and service opportunities are crucial to creating a sense of community church-wide. Do life together. Emphasize eating and having fun as a group. Everyone needs friendship and support. It's an important glue to your plant.

5. *Create an atmosphere of grace and love.*

The gospel must be preached and lived out. Kindness, restoration, freedom, and salvation must be prominently showcased and modeled. Religion and legalism strangle life. Guard against it with all vigilance.

6. *Create a great physical environment.*

We are physical beings and aware of temperature, humidity, spacing, color, decorations, seating, sounds, cleanliness, accessibility, location, parking, graphics, sightlines, bathrooms, and more. Our spaces need to be welcoming, strategic, and imbued with attention to detail. Great spaces create positive impressions and repeat visits.

7. *Cover your church at all times with fervent prayer.*

This is vital. We've had people come to our church and cry without understanding why. We've had people come into our church and get physically healed without prayer. We've had people return to their faith because of the signage in front of our church. Why do these things happen? Because the tangible presence of God touched them. There is so much power in prayer. Never forget to pray, and pray without ceasing.

People don't realize how much work it takes to set a culture and establish an atmosphere. But they sure can feel it and enjoy it when they come into it.

Chapter 10—No Wimps Allowed: Be a Cross-Cultural Warrior

I thought I was pretty savvy in terms of my cross-cultural skills. I had grown up biculturally as an Asian in the United States. I had already traveled to twenty-five different countries before arriving in Vancouver. I was global in my mind-set. But I hit a wall when I moved to Canada. I realized then that living in a culture is different than visiting it. Things annoyed me that I didn't notice when I was just passing through. At times I had to lecture myself on my bad attitude. Getting one's attitude right is a make or break issue; if you can't adjust you should probably go home. We must have love for the people. Jesus had to adjust when He left heaven to come to earth. And He loved the people mightily.

Here's a sampling of things that bugged me after moving to Canada:

- A worship of recycling. Oh my goodness, all that time to sort trash.
- French labeling. Why not just have dual-labeling in Quebec?
- Very few left-hand turn lanes. Cars are continuously backed up, waiting for someone to turn.
- Slow service. Wait staffs take five to ten minutes to get your drinks and order.
- Hostile banking procedures for businesses. Paperwork has to be handled at the location you opened your account. Can't do it at a sister branch. What's the point then of having branches?
- Waiting in queues. Don't move to an open slot unless called.
- Stores close at 6 p.m. on weekdays.
- Running out of stock, even at big chains.
- Credit cards are not accepted at Asian restaurants. Cash-only policy.
- Gas nozzles can't be clipped into the "on" position. Have to hold the handle the entire filling time.

As you can tell, these are life and death issues (sarcasm). Unfortunately, they exposed my personal preferences and pettiness. I was being a wimp. I had to learn to stop whining and grow up. I'm glad to share that with time I changed my attitude. I learned to embrace this is how things are done here. I had to recalibrate. I now enjoy recycling (gasp). I actually enjoy and appreciate the cultural particulars of Canada. And most importantly I love the Canadian people. You have to love those you're serving.

Chapter 11—Polished Stones: Now Accepting World-Class Leaders

God prophesied to us early on that He would bring "polished stones" to our church. When you're starting up and have no core team, you welcome leaders to come alongside and help. Little did we know how polished these stones would be; the quality of those who would join us was an incredible gift from God.

1. Larry and Jean Johnson came to us from China because God had given them a vision of a crossover Vancouver. Despite a powerful compassion ministry that was showcased on national Chinese TV, they obeyed the Lord and moved to Vancouver without knowing a single person in the city until I picked them up from the airport. That turned out to be a divine appointment, and their maturity and faith in the Lord—not to mention their incredible work ethic honed as Iowan farmers—proved to be a powerful addition. They had previously started a Bible school in Albania, planted churches, and pioneered an innovative senior care initiative in China. Filled with mercy and love they were a beautiful picture of Jesus to everyone who met them. Their timing was also impeccable as they were able to join us at our very first meeting. They quickly became pastors and elders in our church. This happened in the first three months of our plant.

2. Kevin and Julia Garratt were originally from Toronto, but God told them to take a furlough in Vancouver despite having few connections here. Why? Having served as global workers in Asia for twenty-five years they were skilled and sensitive to the Lord's leading. They just obeyed. This led to another divine appointment as we shared like passion for ministry in Asia. Soon we became

their home church, and within nine months, we sent them out as our first international workers. We were still getting off the ground as a church, but God allowed us to send a world-class couple into the field. (If you don't know their background just Google their names.)

3. There's nothing like raising up next-generation leaders—as in David, Jon, Keziah, Karmen, Heng-zi, and more—all in their early to mid-20s. David brought great entrepreneurial skills and helped anchor our operations, besides contributing his outstanding music skills and pastoring our youth. Keziah was a multitalented graphics and communications creative with a deep love for gospel theology and the local church. Karmen was a world-changing go-getter, ready to defeat any giant, and a massive prayer warrior. Jon was a highly sought-after, up-and-coming architect until God redirected him into ministry. He finished two master's degrees "on the side" while doing full-time urban work in inner city Chicago. Heng-zi would help us blaze trails with our NGO initiatives. The best part? They loved doing life together—whether it was in ministry or going out for burgers. It was a dream to have this team.

4. Then there was George—a beautiful bookend to the young leaders God brought. George was a professor of finance at the University of British Columbia, taught in the executive MBA program, and possessed both a CPA and an MBA degree. He came to us after he retired, and in exchange for an office, took over our finance department. He made sure our filings, taxes, and society papers were in compliance, and he made sure our day-to-day accounting operations were running properly. An elite athlete in boxing (undefeated in his career, 126-0) and running (second most marathon runs in Canada—twenty-six—in the masters category), George applied that same discipline to his newfound love of prayer. When he joined us, he started praying two hours every morning for the church from 5 a.m. to 7 a.m., including praying for every member and ministry in the church.

Does God know how to provide? There's nothing like polished stones for the sling.

Chapter 12—Incubator: Start-Ups within a Start-Up

Part of how we evolved and grew as a start-up was by following the proven ministries of the leaders God brought to us. One area that opened up was the compassion arena. The Johnsons (referred to in the last chapter) had a powerful ministry in helping the poor and we soon leveraged their expertise into starting a Vancouver Dream Centre which lived by the motto "Find a need and fill it." We ministered to the homeless, immigrant families, refugee kids, and indigenous people through activities like food and clothing distribution, bike clinics for kids, and hosting "Games Day" in low-income housing developments.

These activities soon expanded into extra-local efforts as the collective ministries of the Johnson's and Garratt's (also referred to in the last chapter) inspired us to start new non-profits internationally given their experience in overseas work. Pursuant to that, we started five other NGOs (yes, five) that served the hurting and hopeless all around the world, from Asia to the Middle East. While two of them had a short life span of three years, three of them are still going. During this time, we received over a quarter-million dollar in grants to carry out our social agenda. All this while our church was at the fledgling state of fifty people.

The motivation to start things reflected our incubator ethos, being willing to prototype and experiment as God was leading. It also created a profile for us that was bigger than our size. We were able to take on these ventures because we had leaders who were game to start these initiatives.

All this represented a bias toward action. When you're called to make an impact, cultivating a high-energy culture is important. Nothing like birthing things while you're still being birthed.

Chapter 13 — Claim Your Six Blocks of Humanity: Seeking the Welfare of the City

Early on God put on our hearts to seek the welfare of the city (Jer. 29:7). Being located in the downtown core we wanted to leverage our location. We not only wanted to see our city flourish spiritually (first priority), but also economically and socially.

But before we embarked on this agenda, our first step was to break down the city into a six-block area where we could concentrate our prayers. This would be our little piece of humanity. This would be our "bite-size" strategy to make the ideal real. So we began praying intensively for this walkable area around our church. By our estimates, fifteen thousand people lived in this densely populated section of the city.

As we faithfully prayed, the area began to transform before our very eyes. Columbia Street in New Westminster (where our church is situated) was known as the Miracle Mile in the 1950s. It was the original downtown of Vancouver. However, as the city expanded and moved westward toward the coast, the downtown fell into disrepute, and becoming a place for drug dealing and prostitution. It became a pass-through city and not a destination spot. But all that began to change. After fifty years, as told in a 2012 newspaper article entitled "New Westminster's Urban Revival" (Smith, 2012), the city started making a massive comeback:

> Council member Jonathan Cote acknowledges that the city, which was once the most important in British Columbia, went into a long decline that co-incided with the rise of suburbia. But the presence of SkyTrain has finally spurred a rebound that's apparent to anyone who walks through the downtown. According to Mayor Wayne Wright, half a billion dollars have been invested in the area in recent years, and up to a billion around the entire

municipality. This spring, the city will open a sparkling $33-million water-front park covering 3.2 hectares just east of Westminster Quay.

The city also opened a new front street walking area and began sponsoring a food truck festival that became the largest of its kind in all of Canada, drawing some 150,000 people. Additionally, some of the biggest churches in Vancouver began looking at opening branches in our revived downtown core, and Alpha Canada relocated their national headquarters to within two blocks of our church. Did we cause all this improvement? Maybe not, or maybe we did. All I know is there is a distinct correlation between our prayers and the welfare of the city improving exponentially. And we've had a front-row seat to it from our view of the Fraser River that connects to the Pacific Ocean. We love our six-block area.

Chapter 14—Alone in the Garden: Battling Discouragement

Church planting is fraught with warfare, not the least of which is the enemy's attack on our emotions. The Bible says the devil accuses us day and night before God (Rev. 12:9-11). The attacks can be unremitting and unrelenting. He attacks our insecurities and highlights our weaknesses. It can be discouraging and if not battled properly, can lead to defeat and throwing in the towel.

"I'm not good enough."
"Why am I doing this?"
"Why did God call me?"
"It's too much stress on my family and my health."
"I can make more money elsewhere."

The worst is when we feel alone and isolated, with no one with whom to share our struggles, or when we feel very few will understand us. I look back at my journal and see how inadequate I felt and how many of my entries were overcome with a sense of worthlessness and anxiety. Here are a few entries from the beginning months.

Sept. 22, 2003

I feel a bit paralyzed by what I should do, where do I start, when do I start, where do I get the people, what will work, what won't. I feel like I'm in a vacuum. I'm afraid of failing.

Sept. 29, 2003

I've been really depressed about my lack of productivity. Feeling like I'm inundated with the "nothing-ness" even though I'm busy. Today is a good example—trying to up my credit card limit (banks here start you at college levels of $500), getting the yard cleaned up, picking up kids from school, helping them with homework, troubleshooting my wife's computer, emailing, and before I know it, my day is gone.

Oct. 30, 2003

I need your evangelistic anointing. God fill me, and purge me from the fear of man.

Nov. 6, 2003

Have been battling last few weeks an overwhelming sense that I'm not doing enough. It's oppressing to me, has me on edge. I wake up un-refreshed. I get palpitations.

Then a moment of euphoria:

Nov. 14, 2003—First Meeting of the Church

God blessed mightily! We thought nineteen people would come; twenty-eight showed up, with six no-shows, and people felt to take up an offering—so we took in CN$150, our first offering! It seems there will be four to five people that will become part of the core. One family was so excited they said, "Where will you build the facility for the thousands that want to come!" So encouraging. Of course there will be a flux in numbers, but God blessed with a great start. Thank you, Lord.

Nov. 21, 2003—Second Meeting

Thirty people showed up. Two more than last time. PG! And another couple gave $100.

But all this excitement was followed by the following.

Dec. 12, 2003

Over the last few weeks I have felt such an ongoing angst about whether I'm taking enough concrete steps. It's really hard on me because I have no feedback, and no definite evaluation from the Lord. I wish He could be here personally to tell me, rebuke me, or whatever. But that's the walk of faith. At times this angst has created weird heartbeats, headaches, and funny stomach feelings.

***

How frail we can be. Were it not for His sustaining grace, we could easily give out. But God never tests us beyond what we can handle—although it may feel like it (1 Cor. 10:13). We may feel alone, but we are not. That's the promise of the Great Commission (Matt. 28:20; see also Deut. 31:6). It's not hard to see how we contain His glory in earthen vessels (2 Cor. 4:7).

Chapter 15—Marriage Made in Eden: The Difference Maker

My wife wanted to marry a pastor. What girl wants to do that? Most want to marry a millionaire or a lawyer or a doctor. But a pastor? Unheard of. And yet there she was, one prepared just for me. It was a marriage made in Eden (Gen. 2:18).

I can't tell you how indispensable my wife Memie has been to my ministry—and in particular, our church plant. Her vision, her passion, her feistiness, her intercession have helped lift a load I could have never lifted myself. She has prayed me out of more preacher's block than I can remember. She has been used by God many times to prophetically identify new leaders. She has discipled women, overseen ministries, and never once have I seen her flag in her zeal for the Lord. I've had my moments of wanting to quit, but never my wife. Not even a sniff.

Proverbs 31 speaks of the virtuous woman, but not many see that these virtues double as entrepreneurial qualities, which are so valuable in planting.

This profile describes my wife.

- She adds value to her husband (Prov. 31:12).
- She is resourceful and hardworking (Prov. 31:13).
- She has foresight (Prov. 31:21, 25b).
- She can spot a good deal and multiply her earnings (Prov. 31:16).
- She has a determined spirit (Prov. 31:17, 25a).
- She is kind-hearted and charitable (Prov. 31:20).
- She has an eye for beauty (Prov. 31:22).
- She is wise and filled with grace (Prov. 31:26).
- She is responsible (Prov. 31:27a).
- She is loved and respected by her family (Prov. 31:28–29).
- She has a deep reverence for God (Prov. 31:30).
- She does things well (Prov. 31:31).

My wife is a dream partner for planting. However, Memie and I could not be more opposite. She is random, concrete. I am sequential, abstract. I start with the top line; she starts with the footnotes. I'm introverted; she's extroverted. She is an external processor (got to get in those ten thousand words); I'm an internal processor. She likes savory; I like sweet. She likes variety; I like routine. She says I'm boring; I call her dangerous. And yet as far apart as we are, we are a perfect complement. She is the perfect helpmate. This isn't to say we walk in airy-fairy land. We've had more than our quota of fights and arguments, but in the end, there is such a commonality of purpose and love for Jesus that that is what makes us so united. It's what makes life and ministry so much fun.

I couldn't imagine what our church would look like if Memie wasn't by my side. And that's the point: when you are called to plant, make sure you have the best helpmate Eden can provide.

Chapter 16—Family Fun: The Kids Love This

One of our great fears in planting a new work was that our kids would get jaded, sated, or tired of ministry. We wanted to keep things as balanced as possible but didn't have a clear strategy for doing that. It turned out an important key was our kids became investors in the vision. Planting wasn't taking Mom and Dad away from them; rather, we were doing it together. They helped set up the chairs. They helped host the weekly meetings. They were concerned about how other kids were doing. They heard Dad and Mom's deliberations and concerns. They saw answered prayer. They saw difficulties and heartache, but through it all, something magical began to happen. This wasn't just Dad and Mom's thing; it was a family thing. The church plant became like a "family business."

I couldn't believe it when this began to emerge. If they were away from church due to school retreats, athletic events, or otherwise, they would ask how the the service went. They would ask who was there and who wasn't. They were interested in how the worship was, if the preaching went well, or who took care of which baby. I thought when they were gone, it would be "out of sight out of mind." But that wasn't the case.

I then discovered their sense of ownership was even deeper than I thought when I unintentionally left them out of the loop on "side things" that were happening in the church and they would become offended if they heard it secondhand. "Why didn't you tell us, Dad?" "Well, I didn't know you cared about Ben coming to speak next spring," or "I didn't think you wanted to know about our lease getting renewed." I was surprised. Actually, I was moved to tears. These kids had learned to love ministry and kingdom work. My wife and I were beyond grateful. Our greatest fear had turned out to be one of the biggest blessings of our life. Planting wasn't a hindrance. It was something we loved doing together.

Chapter 17—Growing Your Church to under 10,000: Overcoming Spiritual Inertia

Figure 17.1 shows the size of churches in Canada when we started planting in late (Outreach Canada, 2014).

This meant if we grew our church to between 150 and 350, we'd be in the top 20 percent of churches, or if we grew to 350-plus, we'd be in the top 4 percent of churches in Canada, or in the 96th percentile range. Not that that should have necessarily been our reference point, but it did mean if we grew our church to under 10,000, it would be one measure of success. While this may have seemed like a pretty doable goal, there are distinct reasons why the bar is so low. Canada is a tough place.

NATIONAL OUTLOOK

Giants of Passivity and Spiritual Disinterest

Table 17.1 shows the general spiritual climate of Canada (bolded line). The comparison to the United States mirrors what I've told my American counterparts. Whatever church stat you see in the United States, divide it by half, and that is a good approximation of what's happening in Canada.

We started our church in November 2003. This table shows general spiritual interest from 2003–2012 was only at 27 percent, meaning 73 percent of the overall Canadian population didn't go to church. Not good. From a wider view, interest in Christianity from 1986–2012 (a twenty-six-year span) dropped from 43 percent to 27 percent. That's represents by a 37 percent decrease in church attendance over that time.

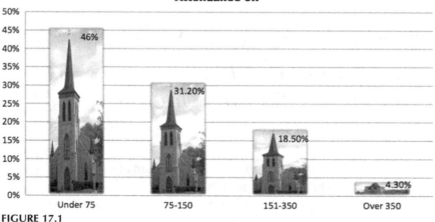

Percentage of Canadian Protestant Churches with an Average Worship Attendance of:

FIGURE 17.1

TABLE 17.1

General Spiritual Climate in Canada (Monthly)

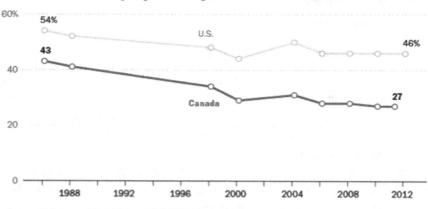

Religious Attendance in Canada and the U.S., 1986-2012

% who say they attend religious services at least once a month

Sources: U.S. General Social Survey 1986-2012; Canadian General Social Survey 1986-2011

PEW RESEARCH CENTER

TABLE 17.2

General Spiritual Climate in Canada (Weekly) (Hiemstra 2016)

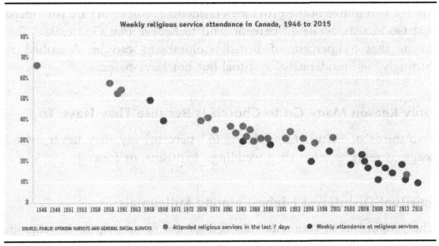

When interest in Jesus was measured on a weekly basis, the statistics were even more depressing (Table 17.2). Less than 10 percent of the Canadian population went to church weekly (bolded dots).

PROVINCIAL OUTLOOK

There was also important data to be processed at the *provincial level* (Canseco, 2019). In British Columbia, Vancouver is the biggest city, making up half of the province's population of 4.99 million. (Metro Vancouver with 2.55 million people is the third largest city in Canada, and the most populous city in western Canada.)

Most Secular Province in Canada

Throughout the course of this century, British Columbia has been the most irreligious province in all of Canada. In the 2001 national census, 35.1 percent of British Columbians claimed to have no religion when they filed their forms. By 2011, the proportion rose significantly to 44.1 percent.

Spiritual But Not Christian

Many British Columbians believe in a higher power, but not Jesus. Almost two in five of the province's residents (39 percent) are convinced that God exists, while 22 percent tend to believe that God exists. This means that 61 percent of British Columbians can be described as "strongly" or "moderately" spiritual but not Jesus-based.

Only Reason Many Go to Church Is Because They Have To

Two-thirds of British Columbians (67 percent) say they never attend religious services other than weddings, baptisms, or funerals.

Spiritual Disinterest Highest among Millennials

The proportion of residents who choose not to participate in religious services is highest (70 percent) among BC millennials (aged 18 to 34) and falls slightly (68 percent) among those in Generation X (ages 35 to 54). Among baby boomers (55 and over), it is 59 percent.

Church Attendance Abysmally Low

Only 3 percent of British Columbians say they attend services at least once a week.

Little Respect for Clergy

The proportion of British Columbians who either confessed or sought advice from a religious figure was an extremely low 2 percent.

CITY OUTLOOK

Then there were salient points about Vancouver itself.

A. Fastest Growing Religions in the Province and in Metro Vancouver (Todd, 2019)

Fastest growing religions in B.C.

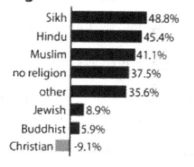

Sikh	48.8%
Hindu	45.4%
Muslim	41.1%
no religion	37.5%
other	35.6%
Jewish	8.9%
Buddhist	5.9%
Christian	-9.1%

Fastest growing religions in Metro Van.

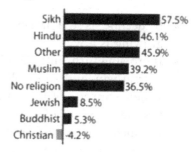

Sikh	57.5%
Hindu	46.1%
Other	45.9%
Muslim	39.2%
No religion	36.5%
Jewish	8.5%
Buddhist	5.3%
Christian	-4.2%

Source: Statistics Canada, 2001 data is based on a mandatory long-form census. 2011 data is based on voluntary National Household Survey.

Here, we see Christianity was not only *not* going forward, it was in decline. While all other major religions in the province and in Metro Vancouver were growing, Christianity was experiencing negative growth at the rates of −9.1 percent and −4.2 percent, respectively.

Taken together these figures paints a picture where the faith climate in Metro Vancouver is so low that the city qualifies as "unreached people group," which is normally a designation reserved for tribes in frontier places like Papua New Guinea. An unreached people group is defined as a people with 5 percent professing Christians or less (Joshua Project, n.d.). As noted, only 3 percent of British Columbians attend services on a weekly basis. Flip this around, and this means on a Sunday morning 97 percent of the people are sleeping in or doing their own thing.

From these various statistics, we can see how powerful the spiritual inertia is here. There are many giants that must be overcome. Indifference, cynicism, unbelief, antagonism all play into a collective coldness towards God. Sin has hardened people. That's why churches must be planted and the gospel must be preached.

WHAT DOES A WIN LOOK LIKE?

In light of this difficult environment, what are some ways a plant can be encouraged that it's doing its job?

- If decline is the norm, then surviving the start-up years and growing is a win.
- If growing turns into 75, 150, or 350 regular attendees, that's a win, a great win, and an excellent win, respectively.
- If new converts of more than six to eight are seen per year in the first three years of planting, that's a win, as that's the median number seen by researchers (Stetzer, 2016).
- If the plant becomes financially independent between years one to eight, that's a win, as up to 58 percent of church are still financially *dependent* after eight years (Stetzer, 2016).
- If member giving is $1,004/year or more, that's a win, as that's the average giving of active church members (Turcotte, 2012, p. 23).
- If disciples are made, baptized, and become more mature in Jesus, that's a win (Matt. 28:19-20).
- If a church is actively and tangibly blessing a city in practical ways, that's a win (Matt. 5:13-16). (Would your city be sad if your church folded up its tent?)
- If a church is helping people get healed and set free, that's a win (Luke 4:18-19).
- If new churches are being planted from the plant, that's a win (Matt. 16:18).

The soil may be hard in Vancouver (and Canada more broadly), but by the grace of God, we are putting checks in the win column. Vancouver is a world-class megacity, but it can use as many churches of every size as planters can plant. That's why we're here.

References

Barna, G. (2009). *Why Pastors Leave the Ministry*. Retrieved from http://www.stevestutz.com/why-pastors-leave-the-ministry.html.

Bettencourt, L. M., Lobo, J., Helbing, D., Kühnert, C., & West, G. B. (2007). Growth, innovation, scaling, and the pace of life in cities. *Proceedings of the National Academy of Sciences, 104*(17), 7301–7306.

Broadbent, E. H. (1989). *The pilgrim church*. Southampton, Great Britain: The Camelot Press, Ltd.

Bruce, F. F. (1977). *Paul—Apostle of the heart set free*. Grand Rapids, MI: Wm. B. Eerdmans Publishing Company.

Canseco, M. (2019, April 19). Most B.C. residents believe in God, but few attend church regularly. *Vancouver Is Awesome*. Retrieved from https://www.vancouverisawesome.com/2019/04/19/bc-residents-believe-god-church/.

Cohen, A. (1949). *Everyman's Talmud*. New York, NY: Schocken Books, Inc.

Cole, N. (n.d.). How many churches did the apostle Paul start? *Church Planting*. Retrieved from https://www.churchplanting.com/how-many-churches-did-the-apostle-paul-start/#.XXnMvlT-RTb.

Collins, J. (2001). *Good to great*. New York, NY: HarperCollins.

Dever, M. (2012). *The Church: The gospel made visible*. Nashville, TN: B&H Academic.

Doherty, W. J., & Carlson, B. (2002). *Putting family first: Successful strategies for reclaiming family life in a hurry-up world*. New York, NY: Macmillan.

Fleming, A. (2011, April 13). Church to showcase local art. *The Record*. p. A13.

Gladwell, M. (2008). *Outliers*. New York, NY: Little, Brown and Company.

Gladwell, M. (2013). *David and Goliath: Underdogs, misfits, and the art of battling giants*. Hachette UK.

Godin, S. (2005, June 5). Small is the new big [Web log post]. Retrieved from https://seths.blog/2005/06/small_is_the_ne/.

Godin, S. (2009). *Purple cow: Transform your business by being remarkable* (new ed.). New York, NY: Penguin.

Hiemstra, R. & Stiller, K. (2016). Religious affiliation and attendance in Canada. *In Trust*. Retrieived from https://www.intrust.org/Magazine/Issues/New-Year-2016/Religious-affiliation-and-attendance-in-Canada.

Hines, N. (2017, January 12). 5 genius ideas that were born on a cocktail napkin. *VinePair*. Retreived from https://vinepair.com/articles/cocktail-napkin-ideas/.

Johnson, R. (n.d.). *Paul's mission strategy in the light of book of Acts*. Retrieved from https://www.academia.edu/10724666/Pauls_Mission_strategies_in_the_light_of_Book_of_Acts.

Joshua Project (2018). Definitions. Retrieved from https://joshuaproject.net/help/definitions.

Kao, R. (2018). *Disruptive leadership—Apple and the technology of caring deeply: Nine keys to organizational excellence and global impact*. Boca Raton, FL: CRC Press.

Keller, T. (2010). *Gospel in life: Grace changes everything*. Grand Rapids, MI: Zondervan.

Ladd, G. E. (1997). *The gospel of the kingdom*. Grand Rapids, MI: Wm. B. Erdmans Publishing Company.

Long, P. J. (2015, September 10). [Web log post]. *Reading Acts*. Was Paul from a Wealthy Family? Retrieved from https://readingacts.com/2015/09/10/was-paul-from-a-wealthy-family/.

Lou, B. S. (2012). Applying principles from 'Scientific Foundations for Future Physicians' to teaching chemistry in the department of medicine at Chang Gung University. The Kaohsiung journal of medical sciences, 28, S36–S40.

Mangalwadi, V. (2009). *Truth and transformation: A manifesto for ailing nations*. Seattle, WA: YWAM Publishing.

Murray, G. W. (1998). Paul's corporate evangelism in the book of Acts. *Bibliotheca Sacra*, *155*, 189–200.

Ogereau, J. M. (2014). Paul's κοινωνία with the Philippians: Societas as a missionary funding strategy. *New Testament Studies*, 60(3), 360–378.

Outreach Canada (2014, August 28). Church attendance. Retreived from https://www.outreach.ca/research/articleid/256.

Outreach Canada (2019, July 19). Church attendance. Retreived from https://www.outreach.ca/Portals/OC/Resources/Research/Attendance-Charts-90-2003.pdf?ver=2019-07-19-051500-213.

Pew Research Center (2011, December 19). *Global Christianity—A Report on the Size and Distribution of the World's Christian Population*. Retrieved from http://www.pewforum.org/Christian/Global-Christianity-worlds-christian-population.aspx.

Pew Research Center (2013, July 27). *Canada's Changing Religious Landscape*. Retrieved from https://www.pewforum.org/2013/06/27/canadas-changing-religious-landscape/.

Porta, C. (2013, March 15). Life of Paul. Presented at Five Stones Church, Vancouver, BC.

Shelley, B. L. (1982). *Church history in plain language*. Dallas, TX: Word, Inc.

Siemens, R. E. (1997). The vital role of tentmaking in Paul's mission strategy. *International Journal of Frontier Missions*, *14*(3), 121–129.

Simpson, E. (2008, April 1). What's the difference between mission and vision? [Web log post]. *Network for Good.* Retrieved from https://www.networkforgood.com/nonprofitblog/whats-difference-between-mission-and-vision/.

Smith, C. (2012, April 25). New Westminster's urban revival. *The Georgia Straight.* Retrieved from https://www.straight.com/news/new-westminsters-urban-revival.

Snell, J. (2011, October 6). Steve Jobs: Making a dent in the universe. *Macworld.* Retrieved from http://www.macworld.com/article/1162827/steve_jobs_making_a_dent_in_the_universe.html.

Stetzer, E. & Im, D. (2016). *The state of church planting in Canada.* Nashville, TN: Lifeway Christian Resources. Retrieved from https://static1.squarespace.com/static/584194b4c534a5709226e1b1/t/5852df6b8419c233346b0bad/1481826162966/New Churches.com-TSOCP-Canada+%282%29.pdf.

Todd, D. (2017, March 26). B.C. breaks records when it comes to religion and the lack thereof. *Vancouver Sun.* Retreived from https://vancouversun.com/news/staff-blogs/b-c-breaks-records-when-it-comes-to-religion-and-the-lack-thereof.

Turcotte, M. (2012, April 16). *Charitable giving by Canadians.* Statistics Canada. Retrieved from https://www150.statcan.gc.ca/n1/en/catalogue/11-008-X201200111637.

Ugo, I. (2012). St. Paul's church planting strategies as revealed in selected passages in the book of Acts. *Global Missiology English, 3*(9), 1–14.

Warren, R. (2011, December 27). 10 key points to remember in 2012. *Pastors.com.* Retrieved from https://pastors.com/10-key-points-to-remember-in-2012/.

Index

Bold page numbers indicate tables and italic page numbers indicate figures.

activation—capability(#3) 39
activation—caringdeeply (#1) 28
activation—clarity (#2) 32
activation—coin (#10) 92–93
activation—commitment (#9) 85
activation—consecration (#4) 45
activation—constancy (#11) 101–102
activation—continuation (#12) 107–108
activation—coordination (#8) 77
activation—core team (#5) 56
activation—creativity (#7) 74
activation—culture (#6) 65–66
Antioch: the new reference point: Acts 13:1 15;
    Acts 13:2 15–16; apostles and prophets (Eph.
    2:20) (1 Cor. 12:28) 16; church planting and
    ethnic boundaries 17–18; church planting as
    leadership intensive enterprise 16; church
    planting as multipicative ministry 18; church
    planting financial considerations 18; church
    planting is entrepreneurial by nature 16–17;
    need for relationship with Holy Spirit 17;
    targets key cities 17; Zech. 4:6 16
apostles and prophets (Eph. 2:20) (1 Cor. 12:28) 16

Barnabas 15–17, 52–53, 55, 62, 83
"biblical-echo" piece 19
breakthrough initiative: David takes out Goliath
    7–8; prototype breakthrough leader 8–9

canvas: Jesus' model of impact—church
    unleashed: activation the canvas and key
    chain 114; carrying it with you 113–114;
    planter's leadership canvas **112**; planter's
    leadership canvas—table, matrix, and
    toolbox 111–113
canvas time, (Col. 3:3) 44–45
carrying it with you 113–114
the church grows up: Eph. 4:13 59; Eph. 4:16 59;
    "fullness of Christ" 59; Gal. 4:19 59
church planting is a prophetic initiative: Acts 1:8
    15; Antioch: the new reference point 15–18;
    "Biblical Lean Model"—small is big 18–21
Coda: God's glory rests on the Church 117–118

David and Goliath (Gladwell) 9–10
David takes out Goliath 7–13; 1 Sam. 17:10 7; 1
    Sam. 17:17–18 7; 1 Sam. 17:26 8; 1 Sam.
    17:38 12; 1 Sam. 17:48–51 8; 1 Sam.
    17:52–53 8
disruption and Paul 61–62
disruption begins before the throne 16

Eliab (David's brother) 12
empowering the whole church: First
    Corinthians 12 58–59; Mark 10:45 58–59;
    Matt 10; Luke 10 58–59

Five stones church: our start-up story and a
    little beyond: claim your six blocks of
    humanity: seeking the welfare of the city
    145–146; drop your nets: doing the work of
    an evangelist 137–138; excellence: pint-size
    churches with keg-size taste 129–130; faith
    markers: God did what? 125–126; family
    fun: the kids love this 152; flywheel:
    throwing two-yard passes 127–128; growing
    your church to under 10,000: overcoming
    spiritual inertia 153–158; have you had
    your napkin moment? 133–134; incubator:
    start-ups within a start-up 145–146;
    introduction 121–122; it feels good here:
    work hard at setting the atmosphere
    139–140; marriage made in Eden: the
    difference maker 105–151; megachurch
    credibility: Creative Spaces 135–136;
    miracles: breaking the barrier of six
    123–124; no wimps sllowed: be a
    cross-cultural warrior 140–142; personal
    prayer summits: ascending the mountain
    to get your tablets 131–132; polished
    stones: now accepting world-class
    leaders 143–144

Growing Your Church to under 10,000:
    overcoming spiritual inertia: church
    attendance abysmally low 156; city outlook
    156–158; little respect for clergy 156; national

outlook 153–155; only reason many go to Church is because they have to 156; provincial outlook 155–156; spiritual but not Christian 156; spiritual disinterest highest among millenials 156

Gideon, Judg. 6:11 20–21

Gladwell, Malcolm 10–11

"Go therefore and make disciples of all the nations" (Matt. 28:19) 103

Godin, Seth 18–19

Goliath *see* David takes out Goliath

"He called His disciples to Himself and chose twelve of them" (Luke 6:13) 49

"He took Timothy" (Acts. 16:3) 52–53

"The headwaiter tasted the water which had become wine" (John 2:9) 67

a heart to raise up successors: 2 Tim. 1:13–14 106–107; 2 Tim. 2:1–2 106–107; 2 Tim. 3:10–11, 14 106–107; "By the grace of God I am what I am" (1 Cor. 15:10) 106–107; Phil. 2:20–22 106–107

Holy Spirit 15–17

"I am in the Father, and the Father is in me" (John 14:10) 41

"I came to seek and save the lost" (Luke 19:10) 29

"I did not prove disobedient to the heavenly vision" (Acts 26:19) 27

"I must be about my Father's business" (Luke 2:49) 25

"I will build my church" (Matt. 16:18) 57

Jesus, temptation of: Eph.1:20, 22 43; Heb. 4:15 42; Matt. 4:2-4 42; Matt. 4:5-7 42; Matt. 4:8-10 42; Prov. 25:5 43

Jesus' caring: 1 Tim. 2:4; 1 Peter 3:18; 2 Peter 3:9 25; Heb. 12:22 25; John 3:16; 1 John 4:8 25

Jesus' Model of Impact, twelve keys of 4–5

Jesus' model of impact (JMI) *4 see also* canvas: Jesus' model of impact—church unleashed

Jesus' ops team: (Matt. 17:24–27 75); John 4:2 75; John 4:31-33 75; John 6:5-7 75; John 12:6; 13:29 75; John 18:10 75; John 19:26-27 75; Luke 10:1 75; Luke 19:29–35 75; Luke 22:7-13 75; Mark 5:24, 31 75; Mark 9:5 75

Jesus said to Peter, "Get behind Me, Satan!" (Matt. 16:23) 95–98

just as Jesus taught them 103–105; Acts 2:41 103–105; Acts 2:44 103–105; Acts 2:46 103–105; Acts 4:4 103–105; Acts 5:14 103–105; Acts 5:41 103–105; Acts 6:7 103–105; Acts 10:28; 11:18 103–105; Acts 15:13-18 103–105; Mark 10:42–45 103–105; Matt. 5:10–12 103–105; Matt. 6:5–15; 18:18–20; 26:36–46 103–105; Matt. 10: 1–8, Luke 9:1–2 103–105

Keller, Tim 17

Key #1—caring deeply: the call of God: activation--caring deeply (#1) 28; Jesus' caring 25–26; Paul: apprehended for Christ 27–28

Key #2—clarity: caring deeply: must have a compelling tangible goal 31; clarity 29–30; Luke 5:16 29; Matt. 6:5–18 29; Matt. 14:23 29; MK. 1:35 29; Paul: called to the Gentiles 30; saving the lost (Luke 19:10) 29

Key #3—capability: planting must be connected to skill, especially preaching 33–34; natural becomes spiritual 34; Paul: dual citizenship 37–39; Paul: equipped and qualified 37; Paul: the tentmaker 39; preaching is prime 34–37

Key #4—consecration: key to your plant 41; canvas time 44–45; living letter 43–44; a man of righteousness and obedience 41; a man of the spirit 42; a man without sin 42–43; Paul: inner life 43

Key #5—core team: finding those who will plant with me 45–52; Acts 2:41, 43; 4:4 52; Acts 2:46, 5:42 52; Acts 5:13 52; Acts 6:4 52; Acts. 6:7 52; Acts 15:16 51; Amos 9:11-12 51; Jesus praying Luke 6:12-13 49; Jesus praying Mark 1:35; Matt. 14:23; Luke 5:16 49; John 6:6-7 51; John 12:1–8 50; John 12:6 50; John 15:15 51; John 21:1-3 50; Luke 6:13–16; John 13:18 50; Luke 9:23 50; Luke 11.1 51; Luke 14:25–33; 9:61-62 50; Luke 22:48 50; Mark 4:38–40 51; Mark 6:31-2 51; Mark 14:10-11 50; Mark 14:27, 50 50; Mark 14:31 50; Matt. 4:19–21; Luke 18:28 50; Matt. 10:38 50; Matt. 16:5-7 51; Paul: assembling talent 52–53; Silas 53–54; Timothy 54–55; Titus 54–55

Key #6—culture: how will this plant work, look, and feel? 59; empowering the whole church 58; new testament leadership 58; Paul: inspired architect 59; Paul the planter 59–60; Pauline church, characteristics of 60–65; the power of small 57–58

Key #7—creativity: planting with genius: (John 6; 15; Mark 10:45 68; Acts 4:13 67; Jesus and 67–68; John 2:1–11 67; Luke 2:7 67; Luke 5:14 67; Luke 6:13 68; Luke 6:28

67–68; Luke 8:24 John 6:19 68; Luke
22:38, 50–53 68; Mark 2:15–16 67; Mark
6:33–44 68; Mark 7:33, 8:23 68; Matt.
1:23–25 67; Matt. 3:20–21 31–34; 15:12 68;
Matt. 4:13 67; Matt. 6:19–21, 25–34 68;
Matt. 8:28–30 68; Matt. 9:20 68; Paul: new
thinking 68; Paul's creativity—twelve
evangelistic strategies 71–72; Paul's three
overarching methods 68–71; Philippian
Example 72–74
Key #8—coordination: infrastructure for this
plant: Jesus' ops team 75–76; Paul:
harnessing *kybernesi* and *proistemi* 76–77
Key #9—commitment: getting the job done
81–82; 2 Cor. 12:12 81–82; 2 Sam. 23:10
81–82; 2 Tim. 4:7 81–82; commitment to
follow-through and execution 81–82; Ex. 18;
18; Heb. 13:20 81–82; Ex. 32; 11–4; Heb. 7:25
81–82; Gal. 1: 4; Rom. 7:23–25 81–82; Heb.
3:1 81–82; Heb. 3:3 81–82; Hebrew 3 81–82;
John 17:4 81–82; Luke 9:51 81–82; Mark 6:52
81–82; Mark 14:36 81–82; Matt. 5:17; Rom.
8:3–4 81–82; Matt. 17:3, 5 81–82; Matt. 17:17
81–82; Matt. 23 81–82; Mt. 16:18 81–82;
Paul: determination 82–83; Paul the achiever
83; Paul the finisher 85; Paul the
perseverer 83–85
Key #10—coin: faith for finances: (Matt. 6:25–30
87–90; 2 Cor. 8:3 87–90; Ex. 11:1–2; 21:35–36
87–90; Ex. 16:4, 13–21 87–90; Ex. 17:1–7
87–90; Jesus and fundraising 87–90; Luke 8:1
87–90; Luke 8:2 87–90; Matt. 4:19 87–90;
Matt. 4:19–22 87–90; Matt. 6:33 87–90; Matt.
17:25–26 87–90; Matt. 17:27 87–90; Paul:
God is faithful 90–92
Key #11—constancy: protecting the plant from
diversions: 1 John 2:15–16 95–98; Eph. 2:20
95–98; Ex. 34:6 95–98; Gen. 3:6 95–98; Gen.
3:17–19 95–98; John 3:16 95–98;
Luke 3:15–16 95–98; Luke 4:18–19 Matt.
9:36; 11:19 95–98; Luke 5:31 95–98; Luke
23:43 95–98; Mark 3:20–21 95–98; Mark
10:28–30 95–98; Matt. 4:1–11 95–98; Matt.
4:6-7 95–98; Matt. 4:8–9 95–98; Matt.
12:46–50 95–98; Matt. 16:22 95–98; Matt.
16:23 95–98; Mt. 11:5 95–98; Paul: apostolic
shepherd 98; staying on message 98–100;
staying outward-focused 101; staying pure
and in good order 100–101; temptation of
Jesus 95–98
Key #12—continuation: raising up the new

disruptors: a heart to raise up successors
106–107; it worked out just as planned 105; just
as Jesus taught them 103–105; Paul: releasing
new apostles 105; Paul the multiplier 106
kybernesi 76–77

Lord's name, 1 Sam. 17:45 12
the love of Paul's life was Jesus Christ: 1 Cor.
13:1-3 115–116; 1 Cor. 13:8 115–116; 1 Cor.
13:13 115–116; 1 Cor. 16:14 115–116; 1
Thess. 3:12 115–116; 1 Tim. 1:5 115–116; 2
Cor. 5:14 115–116; 2 Thes. 3:5 115–116; Acts
9:5, 9–18 115–116; Acts 9:20 115–116; Acts
9:21 115–116; Acts 9:22 115–116; Col. 3:14
115–116; Eph. 3:17 115–116; Gal. 1:15; Acts
9:1-9 115–116; Gal. 5:6 115–116; Luke 7:47
115–116; Phil. 3:5–6 115–116; Rom. 8:38–39
115–116; Rom. 13:10 115–116
Lucius 15

a man of righteousness and obedience: Isa.
7:14-16 41; John 6:38 41; John 8:28 41; John
8:50 42; John 15:5 41; John 15.4 41; John
17:4 42; Luke 1:32-33 41; Luke 2:22-38 41;
Ph. 2:28 42
a man of the spirit, John 3:8 42
a man without sin, Jesus, temptation of 42–43

Manaen 15
Mary: Luke 1:26-38 20; Mark 12:42 20
mustard seed and yeast: 1 Cor. 1:26–28 20; Matt.
13:32 20; Matt. 13:33 20

natural becomes spiritual: Deut. 6:4-9 34; Mk.
6:3 34; spiritual development 34
New Testament leadership: 2 Peter 3:18 58;
Ephesians 4:11-13 paradigm 58; Matt.
28:19–20 58
Niger 15

organizational initiative: it all begins with Jesus
3; Jesus' model of impact (JMI) 3–4; life of
Paul 5–6; phase 1—conception (leader) 5;
phase 3—disruption (global impact) 5; phase
2—construction (new plant) 5; twelve keys of
Jusus' model of impact 4

Paul 15–21
Paul, life of 5–6; 1 Cor. 11:23–27). 6; Matt.
16:18 6
Paul: apostolic shepherd, Gal. 1:6–7, 9 98

Paul: apprehended for christ: 1 Cor. 9:16 27; Acts 16:14 27; Acts 26:9-11 27; Acts 26:13-14a 27; Acts 26:19 27

Paul: assembling talent, Acts 11:25–26 52–53

Paul: called to the Gentiles: 1 Cor. 12–14 31; 1 Cor 12-14 31; 1 Thess. 5; 2 Thess. 2 31; 2 Cor. 5:17 31; 2 Cor.12:4 31; 2 Cor.12:7 31; Acts 9:30; Gal. 1:17 30; Col. 1:15–20 31; Ep. 4:11 31; Eph. 1:17-19 31; Gal. 1:11–12 31; Rom. 1-8 31; Rom. 8:1 31; Rom. 8:37–39; Eph. 3:16–19 31; Rom. 9-11 31; waiting in clarity for clarity 30–31

Paul: determination: 1 Cor. 15:9 82–83; 1 Cor. 15:10a 82–83; 1 Tim. 1:13 82–83; "I labored even more than all of them, yet not I, but the grace of God with me" (1 Cor. 15:10) 82–83

Paul: dual citizenship: Acts: 21:36-39 37–39; Acts 22:27-28 37–39

Paul: equipped and qualified: Gal. 1:14 37; "I [was] educated under Gamaliel" (Acts 22:3) 37

Paul: God is faithful: (1 Cor. 9:3–12); 1 Tim. 4:17–18; 2 Tim 2:6 90–92; (2 Cor. 11:8–9 90–92); 1 Cor. 9:6 90–92; 1 Cor. 9:15 90–92; 1 Cor. 9:18 90–92; 1 Cor. 9:18; 2 Cor. 11:7 90–92; 1 Thes. 2:9; 2 Thes. 3:8 90–92; 1 Thess. 2:5 10; Acts 20:33, 1 Cor. 9:12; 2 Cor. 2:17 90–92; 2 Thes. 3:8 90–92; 2 Thes. 3:9 90–92; Acts 18:3; 1 Cor. 4:12 90–92; Acts 20:34; 18:3; 1 Cor. 9:6; 2 Thes. 3:8 90–92; I know how to get along with humble means, and I also know how to live in prosperity (Phil. 4:12) 90–92; Phil. 1:5 90–92; Phil. 4:10 90–92; Phil. 4:12 90–92; Phil. 4:16–19 90–92; two-tiered system of support 90–92

Paul: harnessing *kybernesi* and *proistemi*: (Rom. 12:6–8 76–77); (Rom. 12:8 76–77); 1 Cor. 12:28a 76–77; 1 Corinthians 12:27–31 76–77; characteristics of administrators 76–77; God has appointed in the church [administrators] (1 Cor. 12:28). 76–77; Prov. 15:22 76–77; Romans 12:3–8 76–77

Paul: inner life 43

Paul: inspired architect, "Like a wise master builder, I laid a foundation" (1 Cor. 3:10) 59

Paul: living letter: 2 Cor. 3:3 43–44; "I am also of Christ" 1 Cor. 11:1; 4:16; 2 Thes. 3:7, 9; 1 Tim. 4:12; Titus 2:7; 1 Thes. 1:6). 43–44; Phil. 3:8, 12 43–44

Paul: new thinking 68

Paul: releasing new apostles, "You therefore, my son, be strong in the grace that is in Christ Jesus" (2 Tim. 2:1). 105

Paul the achiever: Acts 13:2 83; Acts 14:19 83; Acts 13:49; 14:3 83

Paul the finisher, 2 Tim. 4:7 85

Paul the multiplier: Acts 11:26; 19:9–10 106; Acts 18:2 106

Paul the perseverer: 2 Cor. 6:4–10 83–85; 2 Cor. 11:4–6 83–85; 2 Cor. 11:16–17 83–85; 2 Cor. 11:21–33 83–85

Paul the planter: "I planted, Apollos watered, but God was causing the growth" (1 Cor. 3:6) 59–60; "Neither the one who plants nor the one who waters is anything, but God who causes the growth" (1 Cor. 3:7–8) 59–60

Paul: the tentmaker 39

Pauline church, characteristics of: 1 Cor. 2:4–5 60–65; 1 Cor. 4:20 60–65; 2 Tim. 2:3–4 60–65; Acts 11:23 60–65; Acts 17:6 NKJV 60–65; Acts 19:11 60–65; Acts 20:32; 14:23 60–65; bastions of God's grace 62–63; Col. 2:6 60–65; focused on reaching strategic city-centers and regions 64; highly disruptive 61–62; lean and mean 61; local leadership 60; locally-operated yet under authority 63; Matt. 9:20 60–65; as pillars of truth (1 Tim. 3:15) 62; power of God (1 Cor. 4:20) 61; presence of the Lord 65; Rom. 1:11 60–65; self-supporting 63–64

Paul's creativity—twelve evangelistic strategies 71–72

Paul's three overarching methods: "Gentiles-only" 68–71; "Jew first," or "synagogue first" 68–71; "Jew first, *then* Gentile" 68–71; Rom. 1:16; Acts 13:46; 17:2 68–71

Peter 15

Philippian example: Acts 16:12–13 72–74; Zech. 4:10 72–74

Pocket power: key chain for church planters (inside-out progression) *114*

the power of small: 1 Cor. 1:26–29 57; Matt. 13:31–33 57; Matt. 13:33 57; two types of churches 57

preaching is prime: 1 Cor. 2:4 34–37; 1 Tim. 6:2 34–37; 2 Tim. 1:11; 1 Tim. 2:7 34–37; 2 Tim. 4:2 34–37; Acts 2:42 34–37; Acts 6:2 34–37; Acts 6:4 34–37; Gen. 1.1, 3 34–37; Isaiah 61:1–2 34–37; Jesus' ability to preach 34–37; John 1:1; Mark 1:22 34–37; John 7:46 34–37; John 10:41 34–37; Luke 4:14 34–37; Luke 4:32; Matt. 7:28 34–37; Mark 12:37 34–37;

Matt. 11:4 34–37; Matt. 13:33 34–37; Matt. 13:54 34–37; Matt. 23:13–33 34–37; Titus 2:7 34–37; Titus 2:15 34–37

proistemi 76–77

prototype breakthrough leader: 1 Sam 16.7 8–9; build your leadership résumé (1 Sam. 17:36) 9; cultivate a continuous secret history with God (1 Sam. 16:11) 8–9; have thick skin (1 Sam. 17:28) 12; Jeremiah 9:23-24 9; John 17:3 9; know your culture: be creative (1 Sam. 17:43) 11–12; Lord's name as main thing 1 Sam. 17:45 12; love the people, and they will love you back (1 Sam. 17:34–35) 12–13; own your way of winning. You have a sling (1 Sam. 17:40) 10–11; Philippians 3:8, 17 9; see giants as opportunities, not threats (1 Sam. 17:48) 9–10; take a dead aim at the head (1 Sam. 17:43) 11

provincial outlook: general spiritual climate in Canada (monthly) **154**; (Hiemstra 2016) **155**

Purple Cow (Godin) 18–19

"And on the Sabbath day we went outside the gate [city walls] to a riverside" (Acts 16:13) 68

"Seek first His kingdom and His righteousness, and all these things will be added unto you" (Matt. 6:33) 87–90

Silas: Acts 11:22 53–54; Acts 15:22 53–54; Acts 15:32 53–54; Acts 16:9–10 53–54; Acts 16:13–14 53–54; Acts 16:22–24 53–54; Acts 16:25 53–54; Acts 17:5 53–54; Acts 18:5 53–54; Eph. 2:20 53–54

"The Spirit of the Lord is upon me" (Luke 4:18) 33

staying on message: (Col. 2:10–11) 98–100; 1 Tim. 1:15 98–100; Acts 2:21; Rom. 10:13 98–100; Col. 2:4, 8, 16–23 98–100; Eph. 2:8-9 98–100; Five Solas (*Sola Scriptura, Sola Fide, Sola Gratia, Sola Christo, Soli Deo Gloria*) 99; Gal. 1:9 98–100; John 14:6 98–100; Rom. 1:16 98–100; Rom. 5:12, 15 98–100

staying outward-focused: I Tim. 5:10, 6:18 101; Matt. 5:16 101; Titus 3:14 101

staying pure and in good order: 1 Cor. 5:1–5 100–101; 1 Cor. 5:5 100–101; 1 Cor. 8:9 100–101; 1 Cor. 11:20–22 100–101; 1 Cor. 14:31 100–101; 1 Thes. 2:7, 11 100–101; Eph. 5:3 100–101; Eph. 5:27 100–101; Phil. 1:27; 1 Thes. 2:12 100–101

Stott, John 17

Summary of Paul's results from his first two outreach strategies *70*

Timothy: (2 Tim. 1:2); 1 Tim. 1:2; Phil. 2:22 54–55; (Acts 17:14–15); 18:5 54–55; 1 Tim. 1:18 54–55; 1 Tim. 4:12, 6;11 54–55; 1 Tim. 4:12; Acts 16:1-3 54–55; 1 Tim. 4:14 54–55; 2 Cor. 1:19; 1 Tim. 4:16; 2 Tim. 2:15; 4:2 54–55; 2 Tim. 1:5; 3:14–15 54–55; 2 Tim. 1:7 54–55; 2 Tim. 2:3–5; 3:12; Heb. 13:23 54–55; 2 Tim. 3:10 54–55; 2 Tim. 4:5 54–55; Acts 16:1-3 54–55; Acts 19:22 54–55; as coauther of 6 of Pauls letters (Phil. 1:1); Col. 1:1; 2 Cor. 1:1; I Thess. 1:1, 2 Thess. 1:1; Philem. 1:1 54–55; Phil. 2:20 54–55; Phil. 2:23 54–55

Titus: 2 Cor. 2:12-13 54–55; 2 Cor. 7:6 54–55; 2 Cor. 7:7-15 54–55; 2 Cor. 8:1–7; Rom. 15:25-26 54–55; Gal. 2:1 54–55; Gal. 2:3 54–55; Titus 1:10-13 54–55; Titus 2:1, 7–8 54–55; true child in the faith (Titus 1:4) 55–56

"When the days were approaching, He resolutely set His face to go to Jerusalem" (Luke 9:51) 81

"You give them something to eat" (Matt. 14:16) 75

Printed in the United States
By Bookmasters